Mike McGrath

Coding for Kids

In easy steps is an imprint of In Easy Steps Limited
16 Hamilton Terrace · Holly Walk · Leamington Spa
Warwickshire · United Kingdom · CV32 4LY
www.ineasysteps.com

Notice of Liability
Every effort has been made to ensure that this book contains accurate
and current information. However, In Easy Steps Limited and the
author shall not be liable for any loss or damage suffered by readers
as a result of any information contained herein.

Trademarks
All trademarks are acknowledged as belonging to their respective
companies.

In Easy Steps Limited supports The Forest Stewardship Council (FSC),
the leading international forest certification organization. All our titles
that are printed on Greenpeace approved FSC certified paper carry the
FSC logo.

MIX
Paper from
responsible sources
FSC® C020837

Printed and bound in the United Kingdom

ISBN 978-1-84078-839-6

Contents

Introduction

Thanks for choosing to learn with **Coding for Kids in easy steps**. This book will introduce you to web page coding and demonstrate by example how you can create your own great web pages.

Conventions in this book

To clarify the code listed in the steps given in each example, the tags, properties, and keywords are colored **blue**, assigned values and names are colored **red**, and literal content is colored **black**:

<html lang="en" >   <title>Coding for Kids in easy steps</title>

h1   { color : red ; background : yellow }

var counter = 0 ;

Each example is accompanied by a file icon and file name for identification, like this:

hello.html

Check your code easily

You can download a single ZIP archive file containing all the example files by following these easy steps:

1 Browse to **www.ineasysteps.com** then navigate to **Free Resources** and choose the **Downloads** section

2 Next, find **Coding for Kids in easy steps** in the list, then click on the hyperlink entitled **All Code Examples** to download the ZIP archive file

3 Now, extract the archive contents to any convenient location on your computer

If you don't achieve the result illustrated in any example, simply compare your code to that in the original example files you have downloaded to discover where you went wrong.

> ### How to use this book
>
> Each chapter contains examples that build your knowledge of web page coding in the three essential web coding languages – **HTML**, **CSS**, and **JavaScript**.
>
> Chapter 10 brings together all you have learned throughout this book to create a complete web page containing a fun interactive game. Go ahead and skip to Chapter 10 (page 139) to take a peek at what you will be able to create, then get started with coding from Chapter 1.

1 Get Started with Web Pages

This chapter introduces the HyperText Markup Language (HTML) and shows you how to create a simple valid web page.

What is "HTML"?

The first coding language you need to create a web page is called "HTML" – short for **H**yper**T**ext **M**arkup **L**anguage. Despite its scary-sounding name, HTML is simple to learn and is not a complex programming language.

HTML was developed by a scientist named Tim Berners-Lee in 1990 and is the hidden code that displays web page content using ordinary text. It is the standard language on the World Wide Web, and the latest version (HTML5) is described in this book.

When writing HTML code, you add "tags" to the content – to create the structure of the web page. These tags tell the web browser how to display the text and images of the web page. Browsers display the content, but do not display your tags.

The document below has a simple structure of four parts. There is one heading, one paragraph, one image, and one list:

Heading

Paragraph

Image

Bulleted List

The Basics of HTML

HTML is the standard markup language for creating web pages.

- HTML describes web page structure using markup code

- HTML elements are the building blocks of a web page

- HTML elements are represented by tags

- HTML tags label pieces of content, such as heading, paragraph, list, etc.

How do web browsers work?

Each web page is actually an HTML file. These are just plain text files that have been saved with an **.html** (or **.htm**) file extension – instead of a typical **.txt** file extension; for example, **mypage.html**.

When you open an HTML file in a web browser, such as Google Chrome, the browser reads the file from top to bottom. It understands the HTML tags and uses them to display the content in the correct structure. Where the HTML file refers to other files, such as image files, the browser grabs those too and builds them into the entire web page.

When you type a web address into your browser it sends a request via your internet connection to a web server. If the web page is successfully found, the web server responds by copying that page's files back to the web browser, otherwise the web server sends an error code, such as "404 – Page Not Found".

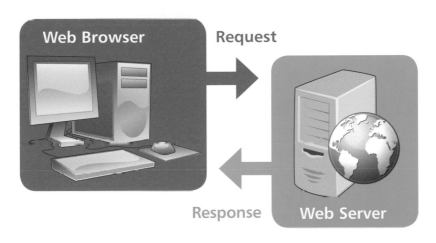

The request and response are sent using "HTTP". This stands for **H**yper**T**ext **T**ransfer **P**rotocol – the system that is used to transmit content over the internet.

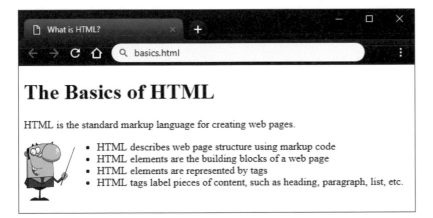

HTML documents should not be created in word processors (such as Microsoft Word) as these add extra information in their file formats.

Make a basic web page

An HTML web page "document" has these three parts:

- **Document type declaration** – declaring precisely which version of HTML is used to markup the document.

- **Head section** – providing descriptive data about the document itself, such as the document's title and the character set used.

- **Body section** – containing the content that is to appear when the document gets loaded into a web browser.

Document type declaration

The document type declaration must appear at the start of the first line of every HTML document to be sure the web browser will display the document in "Standards Mode" – following the HTML5 standards specification. The document type declaration tag for all HTML5 documents looks like this:

<!DOCTYPE HTML>

It is important to note that HTML is not a "case-sensitive" language – this means that the document type declaration tag, and all other tags, may be written in any combination of uppercase and lowercase characters. For example, the following are all valid:

<!DOCTYPE html>

<!Doctype Html>

<!doctype html>

10

Choose one tag style – and stick with it.

You can choose which tag style you prefer but it is recommended you then always use your chosen style. The document type declaration tag style favored throughout this book uses all uppercase to emphasize its importance as the very first tag on each HTML document – but all other tags are in all lowercase.

The entire document head section and body section can be enclosed within a pair of root **<html> </html>** tags. Most HTML tags are used in pairs like this to act as "containers" with the format **< tagname > data </ tagname >**. The tags are known as "opening" and "closing" tags. Notice the **/** forward slash character in the closing tag.

Head section
The document's head section begins with an HTML opening **<head>** tag and ends with a corresponding closing **</head>** tag. Information describing the document (metadata) can be added later between these tags to complete the HTML head section.

Body section
The document's body section begins with an HTML opening **<body>** tag and ends with a corresponding closing **</body>** tag. Content to appear in the browser can be added later between these two tags to complete the HTML document's body section.

Code comments
Comments can be added between other tags in both the head and body sections inside a pair of **<!--** and **-->** tags. Anything that appears between the comment tags is ignored by the browser.

Fundamental structure
So, the markup tags that create the fundamental structure of every HTML5 document look like this:

```
<!DOCTYPE HTML>

<html>


  <head>

  <!-- Descriptive information to be added here. -->

  </head>


  <body>

  <!-- Document content to be added here. -->

  </body>


</html>
```

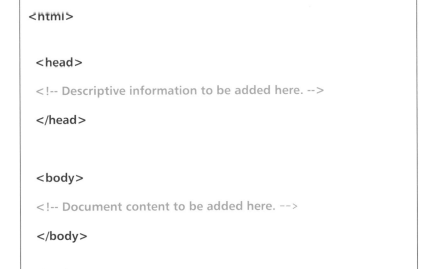

Hot tip

An HTML "element" is any matching pair of opening and closing tags, or any single tag that does not require a closing tag.

Hot tip

The "invisible" characters that represent tabs, newlines, carriage returns, and spaces are collectively known as "whitespace". They may optionally be used to inset the tags for clarity.

11

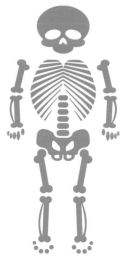

Add web page details

The fundamental HTML document structure, described on page 11, can be used to create a simple HTML document in any plain text editor – such as Windows' Notepad application. But in order to create a valid "barebones" HTML document some details must be added to define the document's language, character encoding format, and title.

The document's language is defined by assigning a standard language code to a **lang** "attribute" within the opening **<html>** tag. For the English language the code is **en**, so the complete opening tag looks like this: **<html lang="en" >**

The document's character encoding format is defined by assigning a standard character-set code to a **charset** attribute within a metadata **<meta>** tag placed in the document's head section. The recommended encoding is the popular **U**nicode **T**ransformation **F**ormat **8**-bit for which the code is **UTF-8**, so the complete element looks like this: **<meta charset="UTF-8" >**

Finally, the document's title is defined by text between a pair of **<title>** **</title>** tags placed in the document's head section.

Follow these steps to create a valid barebones HTML document:

1 Launch your favorite plain text editor then start a new document with the document type declaration
<!DOCTYPE HTML>

2 Below the document type declaration, add a root element that defines the document's language as English
<html lang="en" >
<!-- Head and Body sections to replace this comment. -->
</html>

3 Within the HTML element, insert a head section
<head>
<!-- Descriptive information to replace this comment. -->
</head>

4 Within the head section, insert an element defining the document's encoding character set
<meta charset="UTF-8" >

hello.html

The quotation marks around an attribute value are usually optional but are required for multiple values. For consistency, attribute values in the examples throughout this book are all surrounded by quotation marks.

...cont'd

5 Next, within the head section, insert an element defining the document's title
`<title>Getting Started</title>`

6 After the head section, insert a document body section
```
<body>
<!-- Document content to replace this comment. -->
</body>
```

7 Within the body section, insert a large (size-one) heading
`<h1>Hello World!</h1>`

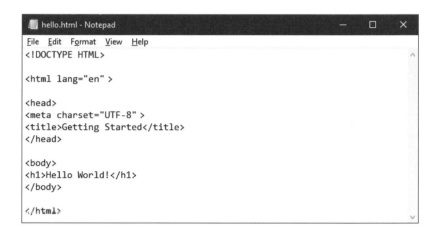

```
hello.html - Notepad                          —   □   ×
File  Edit  Format  View  Help
<!DOCTYPE HTML>

<html lang="en" >

<head>
<meta charset="UTF-8" >
<title>Getting Started</title>
</head>

<body>
<h1>Hello World!</h1>
</body>

</html>
```

The **\<meta>** tag is a single tag – it does not have a matching closing tag.

13

8 Set the encoding to UTF-8, then save the document as **hello.html**

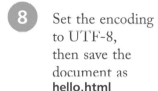
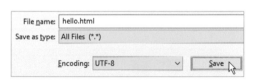

```
File name:   hello.html
Save as type:   All Files (*.*)
                        Encoding:  UTF-8   ⌄    Save
```

You can save the HTML document on your Desktop, then double-click on its file icon to open the document in your web browser.

9 Now, open the HTML document in your web browser to see the title displayed on the title bar or tab, and the document content displayed as a large heading

```
□  Getting Started          ×   +              —   □   ×
←  →  C  ⌂   Q  hello.html                          ⋮

Hello World!
```

Don't get the same result? Check your code exactly matches the downloadable example source code – see page 6.

Test your web pages

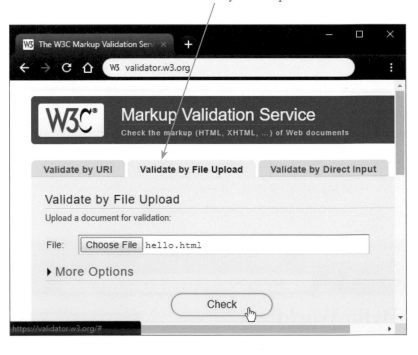

The W3C is the organization that oversees the HTML standards. Their HTML validator can be found at **validator.w3.org**

Just as text documents may contain spelling and grammar errors, HTML documents may contain various errors that prevent them from conforming to the HTML standard rules. In order to verify that an HTML document does indeed conform to the rules of its stated document type declaration it can be tested by a validator tool. Only HTML documents that pass the validation test successfully are sure to be valid documents.

Web browsers make no attempt at validation so it is well worth testing every HTML document with a validator tool before it is published, even when the content looks fine in your web browser. When the browser encounters HTML errors it will make a guess at what is intended – but different browsers can make different guesses so may display the document incorrectly. Valid HTML documents should always appear correctly in any standards-compliant browser.

The World Wide Web Consortium (W3C) provide a free online validator tool that checks the correctness of web documents:

1 With an internet connection, open your web browser and navigate to the W3C Validator Tool at **validator.w3.org**, then click on the "Validate by File Upload" tab

Hot tip

Other tabs in the validator allow you to enter the web address of an HTML document located on a web server to "Validate by URI" or copy and paste all code from a document to "Validate by Direct Input".

...cont'd

2 Click the "Choose File" button then navigate to the HTML document you wish to validate – once selected, its local path appears in the validator's "File" field

3 Next, click the validator's "Check" button to upload a copy of the HTML document and run the validation test – the results will then be displayed

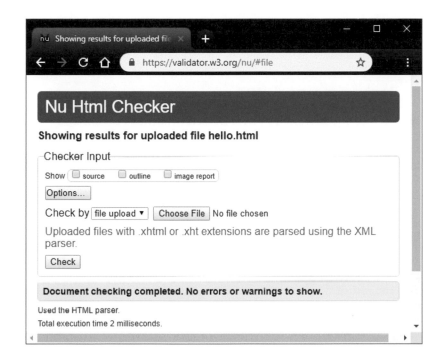

The validator automatically detects the document's character set and the HTML version.

If validation fails, the errors are listed so you may easily correct them. When validation succeeds, you may choose to include an icon at the end of the document demonstrating HTML5 support:

The HTML5 support logo is available in several sizes and formats – find more details online at **w3.org/html/logo**

What you learned

- "HTML" stands for HyperText Markup Language.

- HTML is the standard language used on the World Wide Web – the latest version is HTML5.

- To code web pages you add HTML tags to the content to create the structure of the web page.

- HTML tags tell the web browser how to display the text and images of the web page.

- Each web page is an HTML document file.

- An HTML file is a plain text file that has been saved with an **.html** (or an **.htm**) file extension.

- Web browsers read HTML files from top to bottom and display the content in the structure defined by the tags.

- A web browser can request a web page from a web server and receive a copy of the web page in its response.

- An HTML document has three parts – a document type definition, a head section, and a body section.

- The HTML5 document type definition is **<!DOCTYPE HTML>**

- The entire document head section and body section can be enclosed within a pair of **<html> </html>** tags.

- Descriptive information about the document itself should be placed in its head section.

- Content that is to be displayed by the web browser should be placed in the document's body section.

- HTML is not case-sensitive – so tags may be written in any combination of uppercase and lowercase characters.

- Comments can be added between other tags in both the head and body sections inside a pair of **<!--** and **-->** tags.

- To be valid, an HTML document must define the document's language, character encoding format, and title.

- The World Wide Web Consortium (W3C) provides a free online validator tool that checks the web page code.

2 Create Web Page Content

This chapter shows you how to add text, pictures, and hyperlinks to a web page.

Make a box

Web pages are often divided into several sections. Each section can be contained in a box using a **<div> </div>** division element.

In order to clearly see a division box you can add a **style** attribute into the opening **<div>** tag. This lets you specify features of the box, such as its size and background color, by listing a set of rules:

div.html

The rules list a property and value separated by a : colon character. If you are listing several rules each rule must end with a ; semicolon character except for the final rule in your list.

1 Start an HTML file with a document type declaration
<!DOCTYPE HTML>

2 Add a root element containing head and body sections
<html lang="en" >
<head>
<meta charset="UTF-8" >
<title>Division</title>
</head>
<body>

</body>
</html>

3 In the body section, insert an element to make a red box measuring 340 pixels wide and 100 pixels high
<div style=
        "width:340px; height:100px; background:red" >
<!-- Content to replace this comment later. -->
</div>

4 Save the HTML document then open it in your computer's web browser to see the box appear

5 Insert another rule into the list – to center the box
<div style="margin:auto;
        width:360px; height:100px; background:red" >

18

...cont'd

6 Save the HTML document again, then open it in your computer's web browser to see the centered box

If you view this web page on a cellphone you may see that the size of the box is automatically reduced by the phone's browser:

7 Add another element to the document's head section to prevent phone browser's changing the size of the box

```
<meta name="viewport"
      content="width=device-width, initial-scale=1.0" >
```

8 Save the HTML document once more then see that the phone's browser no longer reduces the size of the box

Hot tip

Cellphones often scale down web pages to fit them on their small screens. You can add this extra **<meta>** tag to all your web pages to control view sizes.

Don't get the same result? Check your code exactly matches the downloadable example source code – see page 6.

Display headings

HTML heading elements are created using **<h1>**, **<h2>**, **<h3>**, **<h4>**, **<h5>**, and **<h6>** tags. These are ranked in importance by their number – where **<h1>** has the greatest importance, and **<h6>** has the least importance. Each heading must have a matching closing tag and should only contain heading text. The heading's text size will reflect its importance in announcing items on the web page, but headings can also serve other purposes.

Heading elements should be used to give the document structure by correctly ordering them – so **<h2>** elements below an **<h1>** element, **<h3>** elements below an **<h2>** element, and so on. This structure helps readers quickly skim through a document by reading its headings. Search engines, such as Google, may promote documents that have correctly ordered headings as they can use the headings in their index. They guess that headings are likely to describe the document's contents.

The **<h1>** element is by far the most important heading and should ideally appear only once to announce the document heading. Often this may be a version of the document title. Below that, a number of **<h2>** headings can begin section headings for longer documents. Each section might also contain article headings in **<h3>** elements, and subarticle headings in **<h4>** elements:

heading.html

1 Start an HTML file with a document type declaration
<!DOCTYPE HTML>

2 Add a root element containing head and body sections
<html lang="en" >
<head>
<meta charset="UTF-8" >
<title>Heading</title>
</head>
<body>
<!-- Content to replace this comment. -->
</body>
</html>

3 In the body section, insert a main document heading
<h1>Document Heading</h1>

4 Next, in the body section, insert a section heading
<h2>Section Heading</h2>

...cont'd

5 Now, in the body section, insert some article headings that could be followed by the article's content
```
<h3>Article Heading</h3> <!-- Content to go here. -->
<h4>Subarticle Heading</h4> <!-- More content here. -->
```

6 Finally, add another section with two more articles
```
<h2>Section Heading</h2>
<h3>Article Heading</h3> <!-- Content to go here. -->
<h4>Subarticle Heading</h4> <!-- More content here. -->
```

7 Save the HTML document then open it in your web browser to see the headings and document structure

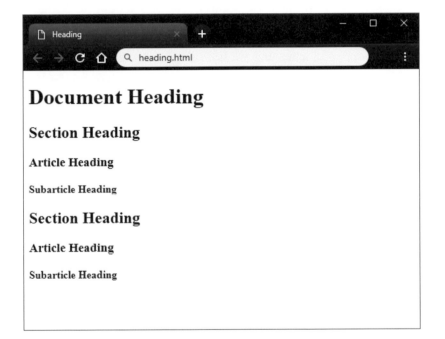

Never use heading elements to control the size of text – always use headings for structure.

The document structure created by the correctly ordered headings is known as the document "outline". Properly ordered outlines allow a part of the page, such as a single article, to be easily linked to another website.

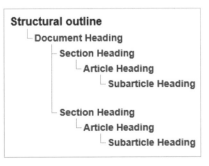

Don't get the same result? Check your code exactly matches the downloadable example source code – see page 6.

Write text

Printed text in a book is usually split into sentences and paragraphs to be more easily read and more easily understood. This is also true for text content on web pages and their paragraphs are contained within **<p>** **</p>** tags. Each paragraph element is separated from the next one by the browser – usually leaving two empty lines between each paragraph.

Text in a paragraph will normally wrap automatically to the next line when it meets the element's edge but it can be forced to wrap sooner by inserting a line break **
** tag.

For emphasis, a horizontal rule **<hr>** tag can be inserted between paragraphs to draw a line separating them. The **<hr>** tag cannot, however, be used inside a paragraph to separate sentences. A horizontal rule should be used to represent a change of article.

The **
** tag and **<hr>** tag are both single tags that need no matching closing tag.

para.html

1 Start an HTML file with a document type declaration
<!DOCTYPE HTML>

2 Add a root element containing head and body sections
<html lang="en" >
<head>
<meta charset="UTF-8" >
<title>Paragraph</title>
</head>
<body>
<!-- Headings to replace this comment. -->
</body>
</html>

3 Insert a large heading within the body section
<h1>The Statue of Liberty</h1>

4 Next, add a paragraph within the body section
<p>The Statue of Liberty was built over nine years by French sculptor Auguste Bartholdi. Upon its completion in 1884 all 350 individual pieces of the statue were packed into 214 crates for the long boat ride from France to New York.</p>

...cont'd

5 After the paragraph, add a horizontal ruled line
`<hr>`

6 After the horizontal ruled line, add a second paragraph
`<p>The statue arrived in America several months later and was reconstructed on Liberty Island. Auguste Bartholdi thought that the New York harbor was the perfect setting for his masterpiece because it was where immigrants got their first view of the New World.</p>`

7 Now, insert breaks into the paragraphs to control the length of their lines
`<p>The Statue of Liberty was built over nine years by French sculptor Auguste Bartholdi.<br>Upon its completion in 1884 all 350 individual pieces of the statue were packed into <br>214 crates for the long boat ride from France to New York.</p>`

`<p>The statue arrived in America several months later and was reconstructed on <br>Liberty Island. Auguste Bartholdi thought that the New York harbor was the perfect <br>setting for his masterpiece because it was where immigrants got their first view of <br>the New World.</p>`

8 Save the HTML document then open it in your web browser to see the heading, paragraphs, forced line breaks, and horizontal ruled line

Hot tip

The `<hr>` element can be considered to be the HTML equivalent of the *** section separator often found in stories and essays.

Don't get the same result? Check your code exactly matches the downloadable example source code – see page 6.

23

The Statue of Liberty

The Statue of Liberty was built over nine years by French sculptor Auguste Bartholdi. Upon its completion in 1884 all 350 individual pieces of the statue were packed into 214 crates for the long boat ride from France to New York.

The statue arrived in America several months later and was reconstructed on Liberty Island. Auguste Bartholdi thought that the New York harbor was the perfect setting for his masterpiece because it was where immigrants got their first view of the New World.

Add emphasis

HTML provides four elements that can be used to emphasize text within the body of a document:

- Text enclosed between **<b>** **</b>** tags is enhanced without adding importance, such as keywords in a paragraph – this text is typically displayed in a bold font.

- Text enclosed between **<i>** **</i>** tags is enhanced without adding importance, such as technical terms in a paragraph – this text is typically displayed in an italic font.

- Text enclosed between **<strong>** **</strong>** tags gains importance, without changing the meaning of the sentence – this text is typically displayed in a bold font.

- Text enclosed between **<em>** **</em>** tags gains importance, to change the meaning of the sentence – this text is typically displayed in an italic font.

According to the HTML standards, text in a **<b>** element should be "stylistically offset" and text in an **<i>** element should be seen as in an "alternate voice". In reality these are represented by bold and italic fonts. These elements do not convey any meaning though, so it's better to use **<strong>** and **<em>** tags instead.

The advantage of the **<strong>** and **<em>** tags is that they describe the importance of their content. Also, these tags are more relevant to suggest how narrators, which read text on your PC screen, should convey their content vocally.

As with many HTML tags, the **<strong>** and **<em>** elements can be "nested" – one within the other – but care must be taken to close nested elements correctly. For example, the correct nested order looks like this: **<strong> <em> ... </em> </strong>** but the order **<strong> <em> ... </strong> </em>** is incorrect.

Don't forget

The HTML standards encourage web page authors to consider accessibility issues in all aspects of their web page designs.

1. Start an HTML file with a document type declaration
   ```
   <!DOCTYPE HTML>
   ```

emphasis.html

2. Add a root element containing head and body sections
   ```
   <html lang="en" >
   <head>
   <meta charset="UTF-8" >
   <title>Emphasis</title>
   </head>
   <body>
   <!-- Content to replace this comment. -->
   </body>
   </html>
   ```

3. In the body section, add a paragraph that emphasizes some text without affecting the meaning of the sentence
   ```
   <p><strong>Warning.</strong> This dungeon is
   dangerous. <strong>Avoid the ducks.</strong> Take any
   gold you find. <strong>Do not take any of the diamonds,
   they are explosive.</strong> You have been warned.</p>
   ```

4. Next, in the body section, add paragraphs that emphasize some text to affect the meaning of the sentence
   ```
   <p><em>Puppy dogs</em> are cute.</p>
   <p>Puppy dogs <em>are</em> cute.</p>
   <p>Puppy dogs are <em>cute</em>.</p>
   ```

5. Save the HTML document then open it in your web browser to see how the text has been displayed

Hot tip

The `<b>` tag should be avoided wherever possible but one legitimate use is to markup the first sentence of an article.

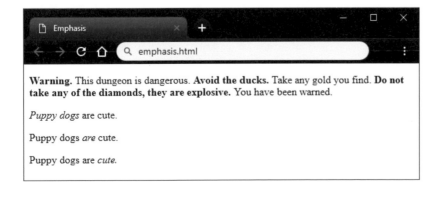

Don't get the same result? Check your code exactly matches the downloadable example source code – see page 6.

Include pictures

The ability to add images to HTML document content introduces lots of exciting possibilities. An image is easily added to the document using the **<img>** tag, which should preferably always include these attributes:

- A **src** (source) attribute is required to specify the name of the image file to be added to the document.

- A **width** attribute is recommended to specify the pixel width of the area that the image will occupy on the page.

- A **height** attribute is recommended to specify the pixel height of the area the image will occupy on the page.

- An **alt** (alternative) attribute is required to specify text describing the image when the image cannot be loaded.

The values assigned to the **width** and **height** attributes tell the web browser to create a content area on the web page of that size. This doesn't need to be the actual size of the image, as the web browser can display the image in another size. You must be careful to avoid distortion, though, by ensuring the dimensions are scaled in proportion to the actual image size. Also, images should only be scaled down, as scaling up often results in "pixelation" – where individual pixels are visible to the eye. It's not a good idea to rely on the browser to scale down images that are not to be displayed full size, as this requires downloading unnecessarily larger files. It is better to adjust the image size to the actual dimensions it will occupy on the web page using a graphics editor, such as Windows' Paint application, so the image will download and display faster.

Attributes in HTML tags can appear in any order.

 Original file size

Item type: PNG File
Dimensions: 600 x 449
Size: 124 KB

 Reduced to 33%

Item type: PNG File
Dimensions: 200 x 150
Size: 30.5 KB

Avoid the Bitmap (BMP) file format for web graphics – saving the original image shown here as **fish.bmp** creates a file size of 790 KB!

The optimum file type for web graphics is often the Portable Network Graphics (PNG) format, which produces compact files and supports transparency.

...cont'd

1 Start an HTML file with a document type declaration
<!DOCTYPE HTML>

image.html

2 Add a root element containing head and body sections
<html lang="en" >
<head>
<meta charset="UTF-8" >
<title>Image</title>
</head>
<body> <!-- Content to replace this. --> **</body>**
</html>

3 Within the body section, insert three image elements – to
display a graphic at full size, plus two scaled versions
<img src="fish.png" width="200" height="150" alt="Fish">
<img src="fish.png" width="150" height="112" alt="Fish">
<img src="fish.png" width="100" height="75" alt="Fish">

4 Save the document then open it in your browser to see
the background shining through transparent image areas

> **Don't get the same result?** Check your code exactly matches the downloadable example source code – see page 6.

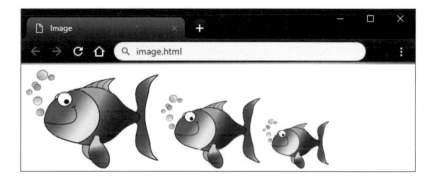

Hot tip

You can change the default background color in the Google Chrome web browser by installing a new "theme". To change the default background color in the Firefox web browser select the hamburger button, Options, Fonts & Colors, Colors, then click Background and choose a new color.

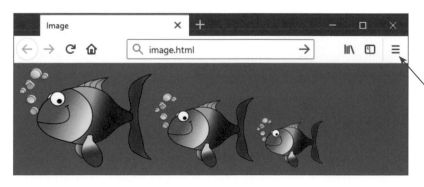

Provide links

When the internet carried only text content, "hypertext" provided the ability to easily view related documents and was fundamental to the creation of the World Wide Web. Today, images can also be used for this purpose so any navigational element of a web page is now referred to as a "hyperlink" (or simply as a "link").

Links are enclosed between **<a> </a>** anchor tags, which specify the target address to an **href** (hyperlink reference) attribute in the opening tag. The web browser will often display a link in a way that distinguishes it from regular text – typically link text gains an underline and image-based links may gain a colored border. You can also add a hint to the link's purpose by adding a **title** attribute to the **<a>** tag, to react when the cursor hovers over the link:

link.html

1 Start an HTML file with a document type declaration
<!DOCTYPE HTML>

2 Add a root element containing head and body sections
```
<html lang="en" >
<head>
<meta charset="UTF-8" >
<title>Link</title>
</head>
<body>
<!-- Content to replace this comment. -->
</body>
</html>
```

3 In the body section, insert a text link to a target page – including a hint
```
<a href="target.html"
    title="A text link to a target page" >Visit Target</a>
```

4 Also in the body section, insert an image link to a target page – including a hint
```
<a href="target.html"
    title="A graphic link to a target page" >
<img src="link.png" width="32" height="32" alt="Link" >
</a>
```

target.html

5 Save the HTML document, then create a similar document containing a link targeting the first document
```
<a href="link.html" title="A link to return" >Return</a>
```

6 Open the first document in your web browser, then place the cursor over the text link to see its hint

Hot tip

This web browser also shows the target of a link when you place your cursor over the link.

7 Next, place the cursor over the image link to see its hint

8 Now, click either link to visit the target page, then click the link there to go back to the first page

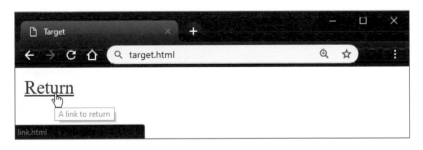

Hot tip

Notice here that the text link color changes from blue to purple to indicate visited pages.

Don't get the same result? Check your code exactly matches the downloadable example source code – see page 6.

What you learned

- Sections of a web page can be contained in a box using a **<div>** division element.

- The **style** attribute of a **<div>** tag can list a set of rules to specify the size and appearance of the box.

- A **<meta>** tag can be used to control the view size of a web page for cellphone web browsers.

- Heading elements are ranked in order of importance from **<h1>** down to **<h6>**

- Correctly ordered heading elements describe the document structure and create the document outline.

- A paragraph is enclosed within a **<p>** element and may use the **
** tag to force breaks between lines of text.

- A horizontal rule **<hr>** tag can be inserted between paragraphs to draw a line separating them.

- The **<strong>** and **<em>** elements are preferred over the **<b>** and **<i>** elements to emphasize text.

- All **<strong>** element text is typically displayed in bold, and all **<em>** element text is typically displayed in italics.

- The **<img>** tag places an image on the web page and should preferably always include **src**, **width**, **height**, and **alt** attributes.

- The Portable Network Graphics (PNG) format produces compact image files and supports transparency.

- The **<a>** anchor element is used to add a link to a web page whose address is specified to its **href** attribute.

- Text and images can both be used as links and can include a hint specified to a **title** attribute in the **<a>** anchor tag.

3 Make Lists and Tables

Display bullets

Unordered lists, where the order of list items is not important, typically put a bullet-point before each item to differentiate list items from regular text.

In HTML, unordered lists are created with **<ul> </ul>** tags, which provide a container for list items. Each list item can be created using **<li> </li>** tags to enclose the item. An unordered list **<ul>** element can contain numerous list item **<li>** elements.

The bullet-point that differentiates unordered list items from regular text may be one of these three marker types:

- **Disc** – a filled circular bullet-point (the default style)

- **Circle** – an unfilled circular bullet-point

- **Square** – a filled square bullet-point

A style rule can specify any one of the above values to the unordered list's **list-style-type** property, or a **none** value can be specified to that property to suppress bullet-points altogether.

Each HTML list also has a **list-style-image** property that can specify an image file to be used as the list's bullet-point. This will appear in place of any of the marker type bullet-points. Where the web browser cannot use the specified image, the marker specified to its **list-style-type** property will be used, or when no marker has been specified, the default will be used.

When no marker type has been specified, the default will be used.

ulist.html

1 Start an HTML file with a document type declaration
<!DOCTYPE HTML>

2 Add a root element containing head and body sections
```
<html lang="en" >
<head>
<meta charset="UTF-8" >
<title>Unordered List</title>
</head>
<body>
<!-- Content to replace this comment. -->
</body>
</html>
```

...cont'd

3 In the body section, insert four copies of this complete unordered list
```
<ul>
<li>HTML for Structure</li>
<li>CSS for Appearance</li>
<li>JavaScript for Function</li>
</ul>
```

4 Next, edit the opening tag of the first three lists to specify a marker style for each list
```
<ul style="list-style-type:disc" >
<ul style="list-style-type:circle" >
<ul style="list-style-type:square" >
```

5 Now, make the final list into a navigation menu, by making each list item into a link with an image marker
```
<ul style="list-style-image:url( go-bullet.png )" >
<li><a href="html.html" >HTML for Structure</a></li>
<li><a href="css.html" >CSS for Appearance</a></li>
<li><a href="js.html" >JavaScript for Function</a></li>
</ul>
```

go-bullet.png
(21px x 21px)

6 Save the HTML document then open the web page in your browser to see the unordered list bullet points

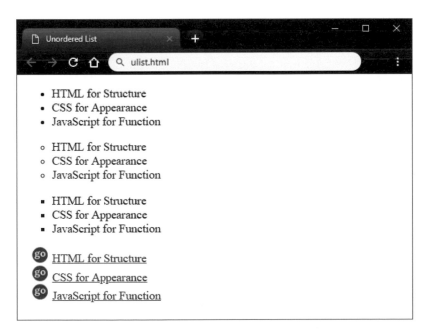

The list items are displayed by the web browser within a content box, and their bullet-points are drawn in a "padding" area to the left of the box.

Don't get the same result? Check your code exactly matches the downloadable example source code – see page 6.

Number items

Ordered lists, where the order of list items is important, number each item to differentiate list items from regular text.

In HTML, ordered lists are created with **<ol> </ol>** tags, which provide a container for list items. Each list item can be created using **<li> </li>** tags to enclose the item. An ordered list **<ol>** element can contain numerous list item **<li>** elements.

The automatic numbering that differentiates ordered list items from regular text may be one of these six numbering types:

- **Decimal** – traditional numerals (the default 1. 2. 3. style)

- **Roman** – classical numerals (i. ii. iii. or I. II. III.)

- **Latin** – traditional alphabetical lettering (a. b. c. or A. B. C.)

- **Greek** – classical alphabetical lettering (α. β. γ.)

- **Georgian** – traditional Georgian language numbering

- **Armenian** – traditional Armenian language numbering

A style rule can specify any of the above numbering types to the list's **list-style-type** property with the following values:

Type:	Value:
Decimal	**decimal** or **decimal-leading-zero**
Roman	**lower-roman** or **upper-roman**
Latin	**lower-latin** or **upper-latin** **lower-alpha** or **upper-alpha**
Greek	**lower-greek**
Georgian	**georgian**
Armenian	**armenian**

Additionally, a **none** value can be specified to suppress numbering. List item numbering will normally begin at 1, but a different start point can be specified to a **start** attribute in the **<ol>** tag.

When no numbering type has been specified the default will be used.

...cont'd

1 Start an HTML file with a document type declaration
```
<!DOCTYPE HTML>
```

olist.html

2 Add a root element containing head and body sections
```
<html lang="en" >
<head>
<meta charset="UTF-8" >
<title>Ordered List</title>
</head>
<body>
<!-- Content to replace this comment. -->
</body>
</html>
```

3 In the body section, insert an ordered list with uppercase Roman numbering
```
<ol style="list-style-type:upper-roman" >
<li>Nile</li>
<li>Amazon</li>
<li>Mississippi</li>
</ol>
```

4 Also in the body section, add an ordered list with decimal numbering beginning at 100
```
<ol style="list-style-type:decimal" start="100" >
<li>Pacific</li>
<li>Atlantic </li>
<li>Indian</li>
</ol>
```

5 Save the HTML document and style sheet, then open the web page in your browser to see the list numbering

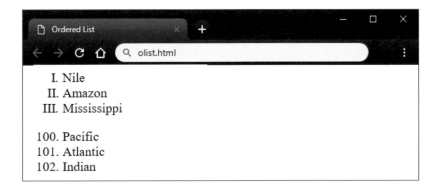

Hot tip

As with the markers in unordered lists, numbering is drawn in the left padding area of the list's content box.

Don't get the same result? Check your code exactly matches the downloadable example source code – see page 6.

Describe terms

A definition list is a unique type of list in which each list item has two parts – the first part being a term, and the second part being a description of the term in the first part. This is referred to as a name/value pair. For example, a name/value pair for the term "sun" could be "sun/the star at the center of our solar system".

In HTML, definition lists are created with **<dl> </dl>** tags, which provide a container for list items. Each list item term is contained between **<dt> </dt>** definition term tags, and each list item description is contained between **<dd> </dd>** definition description tags.

Each list item in a definition list can contain multiple **<dt>** definition term elements and multiple **<dd>** definition description elements – to allow a single term to have multiple descriptions, or multiple terms to have a single description. Typically, browsers display the definition descriptions inset from their terms.

Definition lists are also useful to contain a series of questions and related answers, or indeed any other groups of name/value data.

dlist.html

1. Start an HTML file with a document type declaration
   <!DOCTYPE HTML>

2. Add a root element containing head and body sections
```
<html lang="en" >
<head>
<meta charset="UTF-8" >
<title>Definition List</title>
</head>
<body>
<!-- Content to replace this comment. -->
</body>
</html>
```

3. In the body section, insert a yellow definition list containing two question and answer name/value pairs
```
<dl style="background:yellow" >
  <dt>What is HTML5?</dt>
  <dd>The latest HyperText Markup Language</dd>

  <dt>When can I use it?</dt>
  <dd>Right now.</dd>
</dl>
```

4 Next, in the body section, insert a second definition list containing two list items that each have multiple descriptions – describing the use, pronunciation, and meaning of their term

```
<dl>
<dt>Homonym</dt>
<dd>Grammar: noun</dd>
<dd>Spoken: [hom-uh-nim]</dd>
<dd>A word the same as another in sound and spelling
but different in meaning</dd>

<dt>Mouse</dt>
<dd>Grammar: noun</dd>
<dd>Spoken: [mous]</dd>
<dd>A small animal of various rodent families</dd>
<dd>A palm-sized button-operated device used to move a
computer cursor</dd>  <dd>A quiet, timid person</dd>
</dl>
```

5 Save the HTML document and style sheet then open the web page in your browser to see the name/value pairs

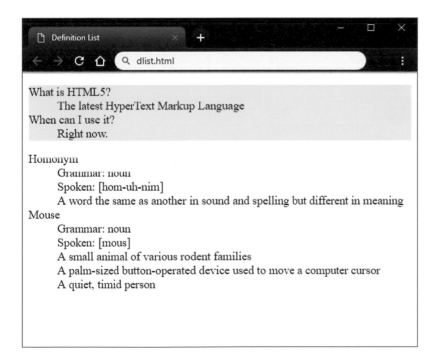

Don't forget

Use the **<dt>** tag for a definition term; use the **<dd>** tags for descriptions of that term.

Don't get the same result? Check your code exactly matches the downloadable example source code – see page 6.

Produce a table

Data is often best presented in a table format, arranged in rows and columns to group related items, so it is easily understood.

In HTML, tables are created with **<table> </table>** tags, which provide a container for table rows. Each table row is created with **<tr> </tr>** tags, which provide a container for a line of table data cells. Each table data cell is created with **<td> </td>** tags, which enclose the actual data to be presented.

If you want to draw a border around the table, include a **border** style rule in the opening **<table>** tag – setting a border width (in pixels), a border type (e.g. **solid** or **dashed**), and a color. The browser automatically adds space around each cell, but you can avoid this by adding a **border-collapse** style rule set to **collapse**.

A **<table>** element will typically contain many **<tr>** elements to create a table displaying multiple rows of data. Similarly, each **<tr>** element will typically contain many **<td>** elements to create a table of multiple columns of data. It is important to note that each **<tr>** row in the table must contain the exact same number of **<td>** cells. For example, if the first **<tr>** row contains five **<td>** cells, all **<tr>** rows must contain five **<td>** cells.

table.html

1 Start an HTML file with a document type declaration
<!DOCTYPE HTML>

2 Add a root element containing head and body sections
```
<html lang="en" >
<head>
<meta charset="UTF-8" >
<title>Table</title>
</head>
<body>
<!-- Content to replace this comment. -->
</body>
</html>
```

3 In the body section, insert a table element that will draw a border around a table that is 360 pixels wide
```
<table style="width:360px;
        border:5px solid silver; border-collapse:collapse" >
<!-- Table rows to replace this comment. -->
</table>
```

...cont'd

4 Now, in the table element, insert three rows that each contain three table data cells
```
<tr> <td>A1</td> <td>A2</td> <td>A3</td> </tr>
<tr> <td>B1</td> <td>B2</td> <td>B3</td> </tr>
<tr> <td>C1</td> <td>C2</td> <td>C3</td> </tr>
```

5 Save the HTML document, then open the web page in your browser to see this simple table

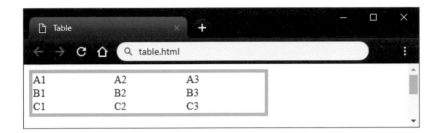

Don't get the same result? Check your code exactly matches the downloadable example source code – see page 6.

A table title can be specified with **<caption> </caption>** tags, and row and column headings can be added between **<th> </th>** tags:

6 Immediately following the opening table tag, insert a caption title and a new row of three column headings
```
<caption>A Simple Table</caption>
<tr>
<th>Column 1</th>
<th>Column 2</th>
<th>Column 3</th>
</tr>
```

If a **<caption>** element is to be included it must immediately follow the opening **<table>** tag.

7 Save the HTML document, then reopen the web page in your browser to see the added caption and headings

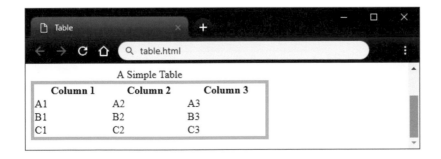

Subsequent examples in this chapter build upon this simple table example as more table features are introduced.

Span rows

An individual table cell can be combined with others vertically to span down over multiple rows of a table. The number of rows to be spanned is specified to a **rowspan** attribute in the spanning cell's **<td>** tag. Cells in the rows being spanned must then be removed to maintain the table balance:

rowspan.html

1. Make a copy of the **table.html** document, created in the previous example, and rename it "rowspan.html"

2. Change the document title in the document's head section, then change the table title in the body section
   <title>Row Span</title>

   <caption>A Table Spanning Rows</caption>

3. Inside each **<tr>** element, add headings to each table row
   <th> </th>
   <th>Row A</th>
   <th>Row B</th>
   <th>Row C</th>

4. In the table data element containing the text "A1", add attributes in its opening tag and edit its cell content
   <td rowspan="2" style="background:pink" >
   A1 + B1</td>

5. Now, delete the table data element containing the text "B1" – as this cell is now spanned

6. Save the document then open the web page in your browser to see the cell spanning two rows

Don't get the same result? Check your code exactly matches the downloadable example source code – see page 6.

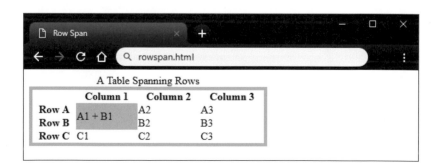

40

...cont'd

7 Reopen the HTML document then add attributes to the table data element containing the text "B2" and edit its cell content

<td rowspan="2" style="background:lime" >
B2 + C2 </td>

8 Now, delete the table data element containing the text "C2", then save the document and view the spanned rows

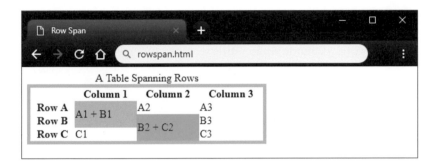

Hot tip

Insert tab spaces between all table data elements in the HTML code to align them so it's easier to configure the table layout.

9 Reopen the HTML document once more, then add attributes to the table data element containing the text "A3" and edit its cell content

<td rowspan="3" style="background:aqua" >
A3 + B3 + C3 </td>

10 Now, delete the table data elements containing "B3" and "C3", then save the document and view the spanned rows

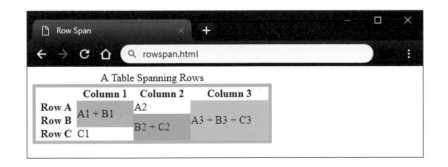

Don't forget

Notice that, by default, text in each cell is left-aligned and horizontally centered in merged cells.

41

Span columns

An individual table cell can be combined with others horizontally to span to the right across multiple columns of a table. The number of columns to be spanned is specified by a **colspan** attribute in the spanning cell's **<td>** tag. Cells in the columns being spanned must then be removed to maintain table balance.

colspan.html

1 Make a copy of the **table.html** document, created on pages 38-39, and rename it "colspan.html"

2 Change the document title in the document's head section, then change the table title in the body section
```
<title>Column Span</title>
```
```
<caption>A Table Spanning Columns</caption>
```

3 Inside each **<tr>** element, add headings to each table row
```
<th> </th>
<th>Row A</th>
<th>Row B</th>
<th>Row C</th>
```

4 In the table data element containing the text "A1", insert an attribute in its opening tag and edit its content
```
<td colspan="2" style="background:pink" >
A1 + A2</td>
```

5 Now, delete the table data element containing the text "A2" – as this cell is now spanned

6 Save the document then open it in your web browser to see the cell spanning two columns on the top row

Don't get the same result? Check your code exactly matches the downloadable example source code – see page 6.

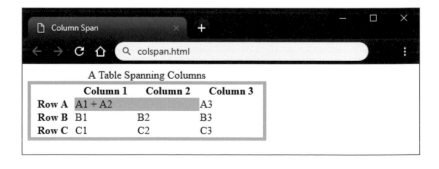

...cont'd

7 Reopen the HTML document then add attributes into the table data element containing the text "B1"
```
<td colspan="3" style="background:lime" >
B1 + B2 + B3</td>
```

8 Now, delete the table data elements containing the text "B2" and "B3", then save the document and view the spanned columns

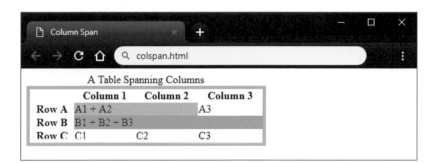

Don't forget

Combined spans are rectangular – they cannot span an L-shape.

9 Reopen the HTML document once more then insert another attribute into the table data element containing the text "B1 + B2 + B3" and edit its content
```
<td colspan="3" rowspan="2" style="background:aqua" >
B1, B2, B3 + C1, C2, C3</td>
```

10 Now, delete the table data elements containing the text "C1", "C2", and "C3", then save the document and view the spanned rows and columns

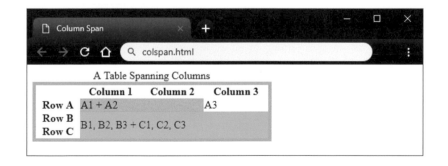

Hot tip

Column spanning and row spanning can be combined to create large rectangular blocks of cells extending over multiple columns and across multiple rows.

What you learned

- The **<ul>** element creates an unordered bullet-point list that contains individual list items within **<li>** elements.

- A **list-style-type** property can specify that unordered list items should have a **disc**, **circle**, or **square** bullet-point, or **none**.

- A **list-style-image** property can specify an image that should appear in place of list item bullet-points.

- The **<ol>** element creates an ordered numerical list that contains individual list items within **<li>** elements.

- A **list-style-type** property can specify how ordered list items should be numbered, such as **decimal**, **upper-latin**, or **none**.

- The **<dl>** element creates a definition list containing terms in **<dt>** elements and their descriptions in **<dd>** elements.

- The **<table>** element creates a table and may optionally first enclose a **<caption>** element to title the table.

- Each table row is created with a **<tr>** element to contain numerous cells of **<td>** table data elements.

- Headings can be added to table columns and rows by including **<th>** elements in the table rows.

- Including a **border** style rule within a **<table>** element can specify the pixel width, border type, and color of a table border.

- Table cells can be made to span down other cells by adding a **rowspan** attribute.

- Table cells can be made to span cells to the right by adding a **colspan** attribute.

4 React to Clicks

This chapter shows you how to make a web page to respond to user actions.

Provide push buttons

Web pages can include push buttons that perform a function when the user clicks or taps the button. The web browser will draw a button if you add an HTML **<button>** element.

The **<button> </button>** tags can enclose text that will appear on the face of the button. Usefully, the opening **<button>** tag can include a **title** attribute to provide a hint to the button's purpose.

To respond when the user pushes the button, you can include an **onclick** attribute in the opening **<button>** tag to specify a function to be performed. There is a built-in **alert( )** function that will open a pop-up dialog box displaying any text within single quote marks, or value, that you include between its ( ) brackets.

Push buttons can also display small "logo" images on the button's face. To do this, the **<button> </button>** tags can enclose an **<img>** element specifying the image, and any text that you want to appear on the face of the button:

button.html

1 Start an HTML file with a document type declaration
<!DOCTYPE HTML>

2 Add a root element containing head and body sections
```
<html lang="en" >
<head>
<meta charset="UTF-8" >
<title>Button</title>
</head>
<body>
<!-- Content to replace this comment. -->
</body>
</html>
```

3 In the body section, insert a button to open a pop-up dialog box
```
<button title="Click to Start"
        onclick="alert( 'Start the Game' )" >
Start
</button>
```

stop-logo.png
(40px x 40px)

4 Next, in the body section, add a similar button that includes a logo image
```
<button title="Click to Stop"
        onclick="alert( 'Stop the Game' )" >
<img src="stop-logo.png" alt="Logo" >Stop</button>
```

5 Save the HTML document then open the web page in your browser and place you cursor over the buttons to see the hints appear

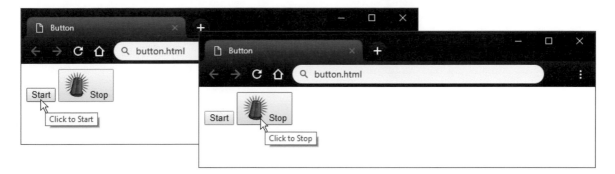

6 Click the plain button to see its message appear on a pop-up dialog box

Don't get the same result? Check your code exactly matches the downloadable example source code – see page 6.

7 Click the button that includes a logo image to see its message appear on a pop-up dialog box

Supply picture buttons

The **onclick** attribute that allows a button to perform a function can also be used with other HTML elements. This means that images can be included in a web page as picture buttons:

map.html

1 Start an HTML file with a document type declaration
<!DOCTYPE HTML>

2 Add a root element containing head and body sections
```
<html lang="en" >
<head>
<meta charset="UTF-8" >
<title>Map</title>
</head>
<body>
<!-- Content to replace this comment. -->
</body>
</html>
```

power-button.png
(100px x 100px)
Radius is 50 pixels.
Center point is 50
pixels across and
50 pixels down.

3 In the body section, insert an image as a picture button that will open a pop-up dialog box
```
<img   src="power-button.png"
       width="100" height="100" alt="Power Button"
       title="Click to Switch On"
       onclick="alert( 'Power is On' )" >
```

4 Save the HTML document then open the web page in your browser and click the picture button to see its message appear

Don't get the same result? Check your code exactly matches the downloadable example source code – see page 6.

In this example the picture button is round, but the image itself is actually square – this can produce an unwanted effect:

...cont'd

5 Place your cursor over a corner of the image and you will see the hint appear, even though you are off the button

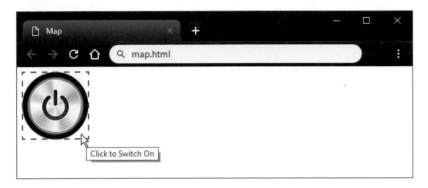

If you prefer to avoid this effect you can make an "image map" to define the circular button area. This needs a **<map>** element containing an **<area>** tag. The **<area>** tag can then include a **shape** attribute, to specify "circle", and a **coords** attribute to specify a numerical list describing the horizontal center point, vertical center point, and the radius of the circle in pixels.

A **name** attribute must be included in the **<map>** element to specify a map name. The same name can then be specified to a **usemap** attribute in the **<img>** tag to link the map to the image – but here the name must be prefixed by a **#** hash character:

6 Replace the **<img>** element with this image map
```
<map  name="button-map" >
<area  shape="circle" coords="50,50,50"
       title="Click to Switch On"
       onclick="alert( 'Power is On' )" >
</map>
```

7 Now, insert an image as a picture button that will open a pop-up dialog box
```
<img   src="power-button.png"
       width="100" height="100" alt="Power Button"
       usemap="#button-map" >
```

8 Save the amended document then open the web page in your browser and click the picture button to see its message appear – only when you click the round button

An image map is an advanced HTML technique. You may never need it – but if you do, this is how it's done.

Notice that the **title** and **onclick** attributes are now included in the **<area>** tag – not in the **<img>** tag as they were before.

49

Identify elements

You can add an **id** attribute to almost any element to give that element a unique identity name. This is a useful "hook" that allows a script or style sheet to refer to the element by its identity name.

The **id** attribute can be given any name you choose, but it must be the only element on that web page bearing that name. The name should be a single word beginning with any letter, but it can also contain hyphens (-), underscores (_), colons (:), and periods (.).

The **id** attribute becomes a "property" of that element, and you can see its "value" (the identity name) using **this.id** in your code:

id.html

1 Start an HTML file with a document type declaration
<!DOCTYPE HTML>

2 Add a root element containing head and body sections
```
<html lang="en" >
<head>
<meta charset="UTF-8" >
<title>Identity</title>
</head>
<body>
<!-- Content to replace this comment. -->
</body>
</html>
```

3 In the body section, insert a button that will display its unique identity name when you click the button
```
<button id="push-button" onclick="alert( this.id )" >
Click to see my Identity
</button>
```

4 Next, add a table containing three images that will each display their unique identity when you click them
```
<table style="border:5px solid silver" >
<tr>
<td><img src="apple.png" alt="apple"
        id="apple" onclick="alert( this.id )" > </td>
<td><img src="banana.png" alt="banana"
        id="banana" onclick="alert( this.id )" > </td>
<td><img src="cherry.png" alt="cherry"
        id="cherry" onclick="alert( this.id )" > </td>
</tr>
</table>
```

Beware

Identity names are case-sensitive, so "APPLE", "Apple" and "apple" are three different names.

...cont'd

5 Save the HTML document then open the web page in your browser and click the button to see its identity

Don't get the same result? Check your code exactly matches the downloadable example source code – see page 6.

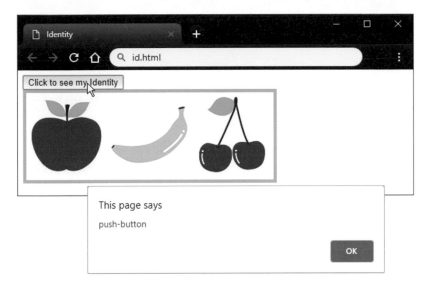

6 Now, click each image to see their unique identity names

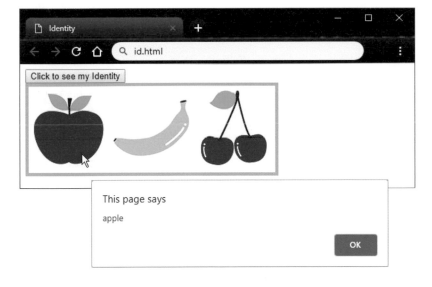

Classify elements

You can add a **class** attribute to almost any element to give that element one or more class names. This is a "hook" that allows a script or style sheet to refer to elements by their class name.

Each **class** name should be a single word beginning with any letter, but it can also contain hyphens (-), underscores (_), colons (:), and periods (.). Multiple names can be assigned to the class attribute as a space-separated list. Unlike identity names, which must be unique, a class name can be assigned to multiple elements on the same web page.

The **class** attribute becomes a "property" of that element, and you can see its "value" (class names) using **this.className** in your code:

class.html

1 Start an HTML file with a document type declaration
<!DOCTYPE HTML>

2 Add a root element containing head and body sections
```
<html lang="en" >
<head>
<meta charset="UTF-8" >
<title>Class</title>
</head>
<body> <!-- Content to replace this comment. -->
</body>
</html>
```

3 In the body section, insert a button that will display its class name when you click the button
```
<button class="push-button" onclick="alert( this.className )" >
Click to see my Class</button>
```

4 Next, add a table containing three images that will each display their class names when you click them
```
<table style="border:5px solid silver" >
<tr>
<td><img src="grape.png" alt="grape"
 class="grape berry" onclick="alert( this.className )" >
</td>
<td><img src="lemon.png" alt="lemon"
 class="lemon" onclick="alert( this.className )" > </td>
<td><img src="berry.png" alt="berry"
 class="berry" onclick="alert( this.className )" > </td>
</tr>
</table>
```

Notice the capital N in className – you cannot write this as "classname".

5 Save the HTML document then open the web page in your browser and click the button to see its class names

Don't get the same result? Check your code exactly matches the downloadable example source code – see page 6.

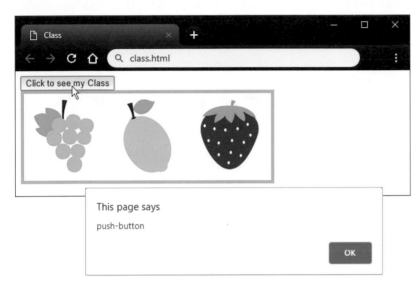

6 Now, click each image to see their class names

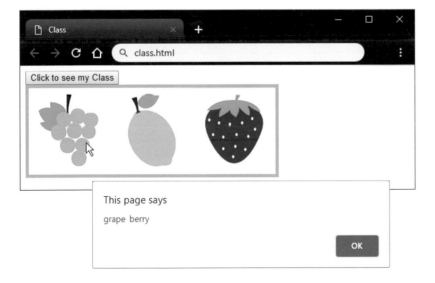

Get element text

You can get a copy of the text that is between the tags of an element from its **innerText** property by using **this.innerText** in your code. You can also set new text to appear between the tags of an element by specifying a new value to its **innerText** property.

Similarly, you can get a copy of the text and any HTML tags that are between the tags of an element from its **innerHTML** property. You can also set new text and HTML tags to appear in an element by specifying a new value to its **innerHTML** property:

inner.html

Notice the capital T in innerText – you cannot write this as "innertext". Also note that HTML must be all uppercase in "innerHTML".

You must use ' single quote characters to enclose quotations within " outer quotes.

1 Start an HTML file with a document type declaration
```
<!DOCTYPE HTML>
```

2 Add a root element containing head and body sections
```
<html lang="en" >
<head>
<meta charset="UTF-8" >
<title>Inner</title>
</head>
<body>
<!-- Content to replace this comment. -->
</body>
</html>
```

3 In the body section, insert a paragraph that will display its text when you click the element
```
<p style="background:pink"
        onclick="alert( this.innerText )" >
HTML for web page structure</p>
```

4 Next, add a paragraph that will receive new text content when you click the element
```
<p style="background:lightgreen"
        onclick="this.innerText ='Set Rules'" >
CSS for web page style</p>
```

5 Now, add a paragraph that will receive new text content that includes HTML when you click the element
```
<p style="background:lightblue"
  onclick="this.innerHTML ='Add <b>Interaction</b>'" >
JavaScript for web page function</p>
```

...cont'd

6 Save the HTML document then open it in your browser and click each paragraph to get and set their content

Don't get the same result? Check your code exactly matches the downloadable example source code – see page 6.

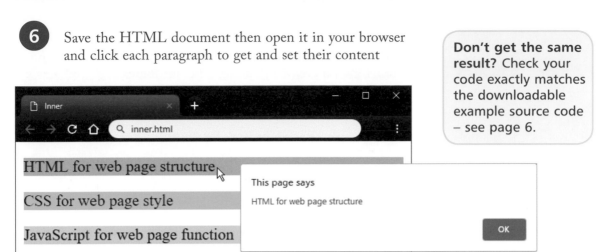

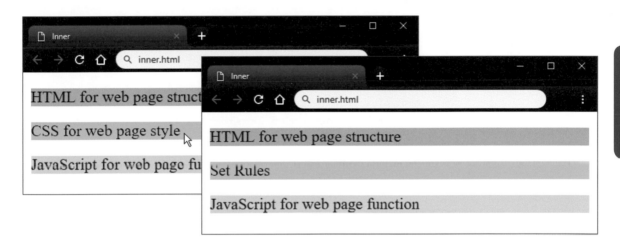

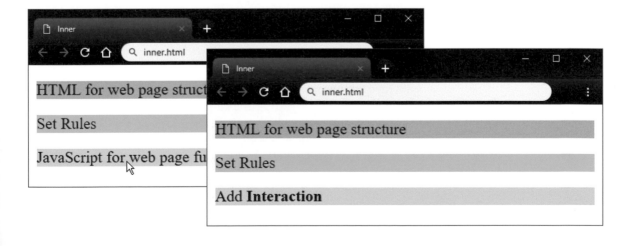

Make rollover effects

Just as a web page can respond to click "events" by adding an **onclick** attribute to an HTML element, a web page can respond to other mouse events by adding other attributes:

● A "mouse over" event occurs when the user places the cursor over an element area – a response can be set by adding an **onmouseover** attribute to the element.

● A "mouse down" event occurs when the user holds down the mouse button – a response can be set by adding an **onmousedown** attribute to the element.

● A "mouse up" event occurs when the user releases the mouse button – a response can be set by adding an **onmouseup** attribute to the element.

● A "mouse out" event occurs when the user moves the cursor out of an element area – a response can be set by adding an **onmouseout** attribute to the element.

Adding both **onmouseover** and **onmouseout** attributes to an element can be used to create a "rollover" effect, which highlights that element when the cursor is over it then returns the element to its previous look when the cursor moves off it.

A rollover effect might, for example, highlight an element by changing the value of its **style.background** property to a different color when the mouse is over that element, then return the element to its original color when the mouse is moved off. You can set its color value using **this.style.background** in your code.

Adding both **onmousedown** and **onmouseup** attributes to an element can be used to further highlight that element when the mouse button gets pressed, then return the element to its previous look when the mouse button gets released.

A further highlight might, for example, add a colored border around an element by setting the values of its **style.border** property when the mouse button gets pressed, then remove the border when the mouse button gets released. You can set its border values for width, line type, and color using **this.style.border** in your code.

...cont'd

1 Start an HTML file with a document type declaration
<!DOCTYPE HTML>

rollover.html

2 Add a root element containing head and body sections
<html lang="en" >
<head>
<meta charset="UTF-8" >
<title>Rollover</title>
</head>
<body>
<!-- Content to replace this comment. -->
</body>
</html>

3 In the body section, insert a paragraph that will respond
to mouse events
<p style="background:lightblue;width:120px"
  onmouseover="this.style.background='lightgreen'"
  onmousedown="this.style.border='1px solid red'"
  onmouseup="this.style.border='none'"
  onmouseout="this.style.background='lightblue'" >
Mouse Reaction</p>

Don't get the same result? Check your code exactly matches the downloadable example source code – see page 6.

4 Save the HTML document then place the mouse cursor
over the paragraph to see the rollover effects

Hot tip

See page 70 to discover how to make a rollover effect using style rules.

What you learned

- The web browser will draw a button on a web page for an HTML **<button>** element.

- An opening **<button>** tag can include a **title** attribute to provide a hint to the button's purpose.

- An opening **<button>** tag can include an **onclick** attribute to specify a function to be performed.

- The built-in **alert( )** function will open a dialog box displaying the value or text included in its ( ) brackets.

- The **<button> </button>** tags can enclose an **<img>** element to add a logo onto the face of the button.

- The **onclick** attribute that allows a button to perform a function can also be used with other HTML elements.

- An image map can define a circular button area using **<map>** and **<area>** elements.

- An **id** attribute creates a hook that allows a script or style sheet to refer to an element by its unique identity name.

- A **class** attribute creates a hook that allows a script or style sheet to refer to one or more elements of that class name.

- The **innerText** property gets only text that is between the tags of an element.

- The **innerHTML** property gets text and HTML code that is between the tags of an element.

- Both **innerText** and **innerHTML** can be used to specify the content within an element.

- The **onmouseover** and **onmouseout** attributes can be added to an element to create a rollover effect.

- The **onmousedown** and **onmouseup** attributes can be added to an element to respond to mouse button actions.

- The **style.background** property and **style.border** property can specify the background color and borders of an element.

5 Get Started with Style Sheets

This chapter introduces the Cascading Style Sheet (CSS) language and shows you how to create style rules for content on a web page.

What is "CSS"?

The second coding language that you need to create a web page is called "CSS" – short for **C**ascading **S**tyle **S**heets. CSS is the language that controls how elements look in HTML documents.

The look is controlled by case-sensitive rules, which can be assigned "inline" or specified in a "style sheet". You've already seen inline rules – assigned to the **style** attribute in previous examples.

Style sheet rules can be listed between **<style>** **</style>** tags in the HTML document's head section. Each style rule selects elements then applies the rules to them. In a style sheet every rule has these two main parts:

● **Selector** – specifying which element(s) of the HTML document are the target of that rule.

● **Declaration Block** – specifying how properties of the selected target element should be styled.

A style rule (or "style rule set") begins with the selector, followed by the declaration block in a pair of **{ }** curly brackets (braces). The braces contain one or more declarations that each specify a property and a valid value for that property, as in this example:

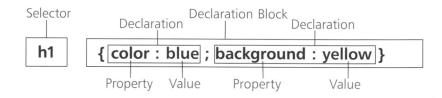

The selector targets (selects) a particular HTML element for styling by their tag name – such as all **<h1>** heading elements in the document using the style rule set example above.

The declaration block in the example above contains two declarations to specify the foreground and background colors of the selected target elements.

Notice how the CSS declaration uses a : colon character to assign a value to a property. Notice also that it requires the declarations to be separated with a ; semicolon character.

The final declaration does not need to end with a semicolon, but some people like to end all declarations with a semicolon so they can easily add more rules.

Add a Style Sheet

1 Start an HTML file with a document type declaration
```
<!DOCTYPE HTML>
```

style.html

2 Add a root element containing head and body sections
```
<html lang="en" >
<head>
<meta charset="UTF-8" >
<title>Style</title>
<!-- Style Sheet to replace this comment. -->
</head>
<body>
<!-- Content to replace this comment. -->
</body>
</html>
```

Don't get the same result? Check your code exactly matches the downloadable example source code – see page 6.

3 In the body section, insert a heading and a list
```
<h1>Most Valuable NFL Teams</h1>
<ol>
<li>New England Patriots</li>
<li>Washington Redskins</li>
<li>Los Angeles Rams</li>
</ol>
```

4 In the head section, insert a style sheet
```
<style>
h1      { color:blue; background:yellow }
ol      { list-style-type:url( helmet-bullet.png ) }
</style>
```

helmet-bullet.png
(21px x 21px)

5 Save the HTML document, then open the web page in your browser to see the style rules get applied

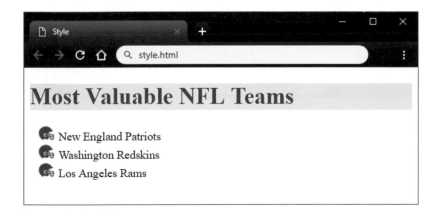

Hot tip

In the name, "cascading" refers to how styles cascade (flow down) to elements contained inside the element that the rule selected – here, from the **<ol>** element down to **<li>** elements.

Select elements

Class selectors

As an alternative to selecting HTML elements by their tag name you can select elements for styling by their class name. A CSS class selector begins with a period character (.) followed by the class name of the target elements – for example, **.my-class**

A CSS class selector can be combined with a tag name selector to "fine tune" your selection. In this case the selector first states the tag name, followed by the period character, then the class name – for example, **p.my-class**

period.html

1 Create an HTML document containing a heading and list
```
<h1>Most Valuable NFL Teams</h1>
<ol>
<li>New England Patriots</li>
<li>Washington Redskins</li>
<li>Los Angeles Rams</li>
</ol>
```

2 In the head section, insert a style sheet with class selectors
```
<style>
.yellow-bg      { background:yellow }
li.red-text     { list-style-type:url( helmet-bullet.png ) }
</style>
```

3 Now, add attributes to the heading and two list items
```
<h1 class="yellow-bg red-text" >
Most Valuable NFL Teams</h1>
<li class="red-text" >New England Patriots</li>
<li class="yellow-bg red-text" >Washington Redskins</li>
```

4 Save the HTML document, then open the web page in your browser to see the style rules get applied

Here, the red-text rule does not get applied to the heading – only the list items that have that class name.

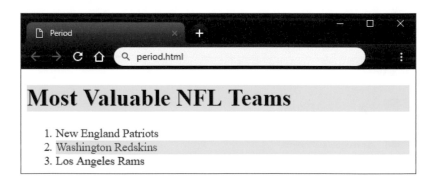

Don't get the same result? Check your code exactly matches the downloadable example source code – see page 6.

Identity selectors

Besides selecting HTML elements by their tag name or by class name you can select elements for styling by their identity name. An identity selector begins with a hash character (#) followed by the identity name of the target element – for example, **#my-id**

A CSS identity selector can also be combined with a tag name selector to "fine tune" your selection. In this case the selector first states the tag name, followed by the hash character, then the identity name – for example, **p#my-id**

1 Create an HTML document containing a heading and list
```
<h1>Most Valuable NFL Teams</h1>
<ol>
<li>New England Patriots</li>
<li>Washington Redskins</li>
<li>Los Angeles Rams</li>
</ol>
```

hash.html

2 In the head section, insert a style sheet with id selectors
```
<style>
#heading        { color:lime }
li#rams         { background:yellow }
</style>
```

3 Now, add attributes to the heading and one list item
```
<h1 id="heading" >Most Valuable NFL Teams</h1>

<li id="rams" >Los Angeles Rams</li>
```

4 Save the HTML document, then open the web page in your browser to see the style rules get applied

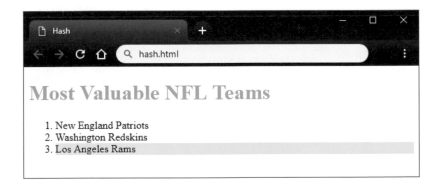

Use color names

Web browsers recognize all the color names listed in these tables. You can use these names in CSS rules to set the color of HTML elements. The names are not case-sensitive so they may also be written in all lowercase letters – for example, **background:aqua**

AliceBlue	AntiqueWhite	Aqua
Aquamarine	Azure	Beige
Bisque	Black	BlanchedAlmond
Blue	BlueViolet	Brown
BurlyWood	CadetBlue	Chartreuse
Chocolate	Coral	CornflowerBlue
Cornsilk	Crimson	Cyan
DarkBlue	DarkCyan	DarkGoldenRod
DarkGray	DarkGreen	DarkKhaki
DarkMagenta	DarkOliveGreen	DarkOrange
DarkOrchid	DarkRed	DarkSalmon
DarkSeaGreen	DarkSlateBlue	DarkSlateGray
DarkTurquoise	DarkViolet	DeepPink
DeepSkyBlue	DimGray	DodgerBlue
FireBrick	FloralWhite	ForestGreen
Fuchsia	Gainsboro	GhostWhite
Gold	GoldenRod	Gray
Green	GreenYellow	HoneyDew
HotPink	IndianRed	Indigo
Ivory	Khaki	Lavender
LavenderBlush	LawnGreen	LemonChiffon
LightBlue	LightCoral	LightCyan

LightGoldenRodYellow	LightGray	LightGreen
LightPink	LightSalmon	LightSeaGreen
LightSkyBlue	LightSlateGray	LightSteelBlue
LightYellow	Lime	LimeGreen
Linen	Magenta	Maroon
MediumAquamarine	MediumBlue	MediumOrchid
MediumPurple	MediumSeaGreen	MediumSlateBlue
MediumSpringGreen	MediumTurquoise	MediumVioletRed
MidnightBlue	MintCream	MistyRose
Moccasin	NavajoWhite	Navy
OldLace	Olive	OliveDrab
Orange	OrangeRed	Orchid
PaleGoldenRod	PaleGreen	PaleTurquoise
PaleVioletRed	PapayaWhip	PeachPuff
Peru	Pink	Plum
PowderBlue	Purple	RebeccaPurple
Red	RosyBrown	RoyalBlue
SaddleBrown	Salmon	SandyBrown
SeaGreen	SeaShell	Sienna
Silver	SkyBlue	SlateBlue
SlateGray	Snow	SpringGreen
SteelBlue	Tan	Teal
Thistle	Tomato	Turquoise
Violet	Wheat	White
WhiteSmoke	Yellow	YellowGreen

Hot tip

Colors can also be written as hexadecimal numbers. For example, the color red is hexadecimal #FF0000. You can find a comprehensive list of these in the Handy Reference section of this book on pages 184-186.

Choose text fonts

CSS allows you to control the look of text in many ways. You can create style rules to make the text bold or italic, specify the text size, and choose a font "family" from one of those listed below:

Font Family	Description	Example
serif	Letters with serif decorations at their ends	**Times New Roman**
sans-serif	Letters without serif decorations	**Arial**
monospace	Letters of fixed width	**Courier**
cursive	Letters like hand-written text	**Segoe Script**
fantasy	Letters that look like graphics	**Castellar**

Hot tip

The weight (**bold**) and style (**italic**) values can appear in any order at the beginning of the list. If they are missing the web browser uses its normal values for them.

Style rules control the look of text by setting values of an element's **font** property. You can make the text bold with a **font:bold** rule or italic with a **font:italic** style rule. Boldness is the font "weight", and italic is the font "style".

The text size can be set as a height in points (**pt**) or using keywords. Where you want to choose a font family you must also set the size.

Keyword	Equivalent
xx-large	24 pt
x-large	17 pt
large	13.5 pt
medium	12 pt
small	10.5 pt
x-small	7.5 pt
xx-small	7 pt

A style rule can suggest a particular font by naming a font (between quote marks) before the font family. In this case the named font and font family name must be separated by a comma. The web browser will first try to apply the named font, but if it can't be found a font of the chosen family will be applied.

All these options can be specified in a single **font** style rule as a space-separated list, but the end of the list must specify the size then the font family – in that order. You cannot specify individual **font** properties of the same element in separate style rules, as each rule will simply overwrite the previous rule.

...cont'd

1 Create an HTML document containing a list

```
<ol>
<li id="serf" >Serif Font</li>
<li id="sans" >Sans-Serif Font</li>
<li id="mono" >Monospace Font</li>
<li id="curs" >Cursive Font</li>
<li id="fant" >Fantasy Font</li>
<li id="sego" >Italic Bold Named Font</li>
</ol>
```

<!..
HTML
font.html

2 In the head section, insert a style sheet that chooses the size and text font families for five list items

```
<style>
li#serf  { font: large serif }
li#sans { font: large sans-serif }
li#mono { font: large monospace }
li#curs  { font: large cursive }
li#fant  { font: large fantasy }
</style>
```

3 Now, add a rule to the style sheet that sets the font style, weight, size, and suggests a named font and a font family for the final list item

```
li#sego { font: italic bold large "Segoe Script",cursive }
```

4 Save the HTML document, then open the web page in your browser to see the style rules get applied

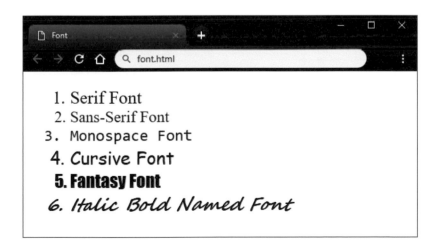

Don't get the same result? Check your code exactly matches the downloadable example source code – see page 6.

67

Center content

Web browsers usually set some of their own default styles for a web page that sometimes add margins, padding, and borders. Often you may not want this, so a style rule can be used to remove any default styles to better control your content.

A content box, such as a **<div>** or **<table>** element, can be centered on the page by setting its **margin** property to **auto**.

Text can be positioned horizontally inside an element by setting its **text-align** property to **left**, **center**, or **right**.

Text can be positioned vertically inside an element by setting its **vertical-align** property to **top**, **middle**, or **bottom**.

align.html

1. Create an HTML document containing a table
```
<table style="border:5px solid silver" >
<tr>    <td id="top" >Top Text</td>
        <td id="mid" >Middle Text</td>
        <td id="btm" >Bottom Text</td>          </tr>
</table
```

2. In the head section, insert a style sheet that sets the size and background color of the table
```
<style>
table    { width:360px; height:120px; background:yellow }
</style>
```

3. Save the HTML document, then open it in your browser to see that a default margin area appears around the table

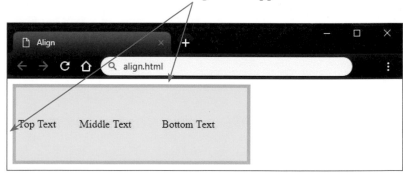

Don't get the same result? Check your code exactly matches the downloadable example source code – see page 6.

4. Next, add a rule to the style sheet to remove default styles
html,body { margin:0px; padding:0px; border:0px }

...cont'd

5 Now, add a rule to the style sheet to center the table
table { margin:auto }

6 Save the HTML document again, then refresh your browser to see margins removed and the table centered

You could combine all these table style rules into a single rule – but remember to include a semicolon after each property/value pair.

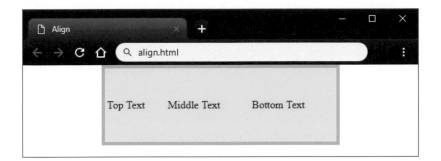

7 Next, add a rule to the style sheet to horizontally center the text in each table cell
table { text-align:center }

8 Now, add rules to the style sheet to vertically position the text in each table cell
td#top { vertical-align:top }
td#mid { vertical-align:middle }
td#btm { vertical-align:bottom }

9 Save the HTML document once more, then refresh your browser to see the table text positioned

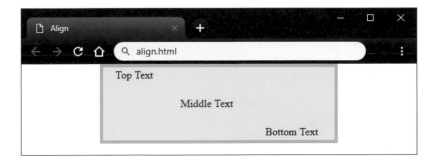

Style backgrounds

You can set the foreground and background colors of an HTML element using any of the color names listed on pages 64-65 as the value of the element's **color** and **background** properties.

Additionally, you can set an image to be the background of an element by including the image file name quoted between the brackets of **url( )** as the value of the **background** property.

Setting both background color and image in a style rule allows a background color to "shine through" an image that has a transparent part. A style rule can also have two coordinates that specify the position of the element's background image.

Style rules can respond to "mouse over" events by adding a **:hover** "pseudo class" to the end of the selector, and can respond to "mouse down" events by adding **:active** to the end of the selector. These can be used to create a rollover effect by changing the background color, background image, or both color and image:

HTML

hover.html

1 Create an HTML document containing a table
```
<table>
<tr>    <td id="color" > </td>
        <td id="image" > </td> </tr>
</table>
```

2 In the head section, insert a style sheet that sets the size of the table cells
```
<style>
td        { width:150px; height:50px }
</style>
```

Don't
forget

It is more efficient to use a single image and swap its position rather than use two separate images.

3 Make an image with a transparent background – the same width as the table cells but double their height

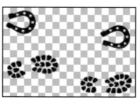

steps.png
(150px x 100px)

...cont'd

4 Next, add rules to the style sheet to set the first cell's background color and respond to mouse events

```
td#color        { background:lightblue }
td#color:hover  { background:lightgreen }
td#color:active { background:pink }
```

5 Now, add rules to the style sheet to set the second cell's background color and image and respond to mouse events

```
td#image {
        background:url( steps.png ) 0px 0px lightblue }
td#image:hover {
        background:url( steps.png ) 0px -50px lightgreen }
td#image:active {
        background:url( steps.png ) 0px -50px pink }
```

6 Save the HTML document, then open it in your browser and put your cursor over the cells to see the rollover effect

> **Don't get the same result?** Check your code exactly matches the downloadable example source code – see page 6.

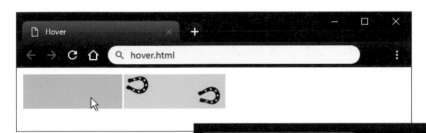

7 Click the cells to change the backgrounds

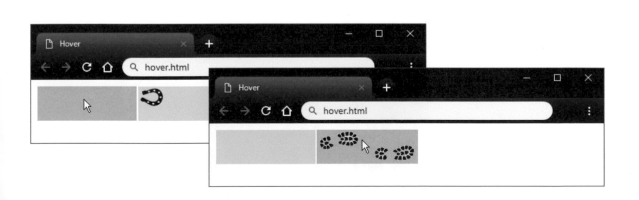

71

Control visibility

Mostly you will want all content on the web page to be visible to the user, but sometimes you may want to include hidden content that can be made visible when needed. This is easily done using the **visibility** property of an element. Setting its value to **hidden** will hide the element, and setting it to **visible** will make it appear:

visible.html

jack.png
(120px x 120px)

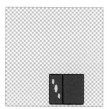

box.png
(120px x 120px)

1 Create an HTML document containing a table that has a transparent image in each cell

```
<table>
<tr>
<td class="box" id="box1" >
<img class="jack" id="jack1" src="jack.png" alt="Jack" >
</td>
<td class="box" id="box2" >
<img class="jack" id="jack2" src="jack.png" alt="Jack" >
</td>
<td class="box" id="box3" >
<img class="jack" id="jack3" src="jack.png" alt="Jack" >
</td>
</tr>
</table>
```

2 In the head section, insert a style sheet that sets the size and color of the table – and puts a transparent image on the background of each cell without default borders

```
<style>
table   { width:360px; height:120px;
            background:wheat; border-collapse:collapse }
td      { border:5px dashed silver;
            background:url( box.png ) }
</style>
```

3 Save the HTML document, then open it in your browser to see all the images in each table cell

...cont'd

4 Next, add a rule to the style sheet to hide all images of a named class

img.jack   **{ visibility: hidden }**

5 Now, add a rule to the style sheet to hide a table cell of a named identity

td#box1   **{ visibility: hidden }**

6 Save the HTML document again, then refresh your web browser to see that some images are now hidden

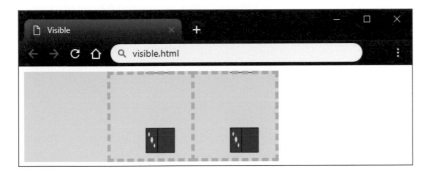

7 Add another rule to the bottom of the style sheet to make one hidden image visible

img#jack3   **{ visibility: visible }**

8 Save the HTML document once more, then refresh your web browser to see a hidden image reappear

Don't get the same result? Check your code exactly matches the downloadable example source code – see page 6.

What you learned

- "CSS" stands for Cascading Style Sheets.

- Style sheet rules can be listed between **<style>** **</style>** tags in the head section of an HTML document.

- Every style sheet rule has a selector followed by a declaration block in a pair of curly brackets.

- A style sheet declaration uses a : colon character to assign a value to a property.

- Each declaration must end with a ; semicolon character – except for the final declaration in the declaration block.

- A CSS selector can target HTML elements by their tag name, or by their class name, or by their identity name.

- A class selector puts a period (.) before the class name.

- An identity selector puts a hash (#) before the id name.

- Web browsers recognize many standard color names that can be used in style rules to specify element colors.

- Style rules can use the **font** property to make text bold or italic, specify the text size, and choose a font family.

- A content box element can be centered on the page by setting its **margin** property to **auto**.

- Text can be positioned horizontally by its **text-align** property and can be positioned vertically by its **vertical-align** property.

- The **background** property can specify the background color of an element and set a background image for an element.

- The **color** property sets the foreground color of an element.

- Style rules can respond to mouse events by adding **:hover** and **:active** pseudo classes to the end of a selector.

- The **visibility** property can be used to hide and reveal an element on a web page.

6

Get Started with Scripts

This chapter introduces the JavaScript (JS) language, then shows you how to store data and perform simple operations on a web page.

What is "JavaScript"?

The third coding language that you need to create a web page is called "JavaScript". This is a programming language that can be used to provide functionality on a web page.

JavaScript code is interpreted by an "engine" that is built into the web browser. It treats the elements on a web page as objects that it can manipulate to provide an interactive user experience. You have already seen JavaScript code in action – assigned to the **onclick** attribute in some previous examples.

The JavaScript language has a number of keywords, such as those listed in the table below, which must be avoided when choosing names in your code:

Keywords:	Description:
var	Declares a variable in which to store data
typeof	Describes the type of data stored in a variable
true	A positive "yes" Boolean value
false	A negative "no" Boolean value
if	Tests a condition and executes code if true
else	Executes alternative code if a tested condition is found to be false
while	Executes code while a tested condition remains true
function	Defines a block of code to execute when the function gets called in the script
return	Specifies a value to return from a function to the code that called the function
for in	Loops through the properties of an object
this	References the object to which it belongs
null	No value whatsoever

Beware

JavaScript is a case-sensitive language where, for example, **VAR**, **Var**, and **var** are regarded as different words – of these three, only **var** is a keyword. Likewise, the object names that begin with a capital letter must be correctly capitalized.

There are other keywords, reserved words, and object names that must also be avoided when choosing names in your code. You can find a more comprehensive list of these in the Handy Reference section of this book on page 176.

Add a Script

1 Start an HTML file with a document type declaration
`<!DOCTYPE HTML>`

script.html

2 Add a root element containing head and body sections
```
<html lang="en" >
<head>
<meta charset="UTF-8" >
<title>Script</title>
</head>
<body>
<!-- Content to replace this comment. -->

<!-- Script to replace this comment. -->
</body>
</html>
```

Be sure to use the correct capitalization or the script will not work.

3 At the start of the body section, insert an empty paragraph that is just set with an identity name
`<p id="msg" ></p>`

4 At the end of the body section (just before its closing tag) insert this script element
```
<script>

// Code to replace this comment.

</script>
```

Single line comments begin with // in JavaScript. You can also write multi-line comments between /* and */.

5 In the script element, precisely write this statement to insert text into the paragraph element
`document.getElementById( "msg" ).innerText = "Welcome!" ;`

6 Save the HTML document then open the web page in your browser to see text written into the paragraph

Each JavaScript statement must end with a ; semicolon.

Don't get the same result? Check your code exactly matches the downloadable example source code – see page 6.

Store data

JavaScript, like all other programming languages, uses "variables". These are containers in which data can be stored and retrieved later. Unlike most other programming languages, JavaScript variables are easy to use because they can contain any type of data:

Data Type:	Example:	Description:
boolean	**true**	A true (1) or false (0) value
number	**100** **3.25**	An integer (whole number) or A floating-point (decimal) number
string	**"M"** **"Hello World!"**	A single character or A string of characters, with spaces
function	**init** **fido.bark**	A user-defined function or A user-defined object method
object	**fido** **document**	A user-defined object or A built-in object

A JavaScript variable is created using the **var** keyword followed by a space and a name of your choice. The variable name can include letters, numbers, and underscore characters – but can't include spaces or begin with a number. You must also avoid the JavaScript keywords, reserved words, and object names listed on page 176.

After creating ("declaring") a variable, the script can later assign a value to be stored in that variable. Alternatively, a variable may be assigned when creating the variable. When a value has been stored in a variable, that variable is said to have been "initialized":

```
var myNumber ;                    // Create a variable.
myNumber = 10 ;                   // Initialize a variable.
var myString = "Hello World!" ;   // Create and initialize a variable.
```

Multiple variables may be declared on a single line too:

```
var i , j , k ;                   // Create 3 variables.
var num =10 , char = "C" ;        // Create and initialize 2 variables.
```

Upon initialization JavaScript automatically sets the variable type for the value assigned. Assigning a different data type later in the script changes the variable type. The current variable type can be seen using the **typeof** keyword.

A variable name acts like an alias for the value it contains – using the name in a script gets its stored value.

Choose meaningful names for your variables – it makes the script easier to understand later on.

78

1 Create an HTML document that has an empty paragraph and a script element

```
<p id="msg" ></p>

<script>

// Code to replace this comment.

</script>
```

type.html

2 In the script element, write these lines of code to create and initialize variables of different data types

```
var str = "Text Content in JavaScript" ;
var num = 100 ;
var bln = true ;
var fcn = alert ;
var obj = document.getElementById( "msg" ) ;
```

3 Now, add these lines of code to write the variable values and their data types into the paragraph

```
obj.innerHTML   = str + "..." + typeof str + "<br>" ;
obj.innerHTML += num + "..." + typeof num + "<br>" ;
obj.innerHTML += bln + "..." + typeof bln + "<br>" ;
obj.innerHTML += fcn + "..." + typeof fcn  + "<br>" ;
obj.innerHTML += obj + "..." + typeof obj + "<br>" ;
```

The **typeof** keyword says "undefined" for uninitialized variables.

4 Save the HTML document then open the web page in your browser to see the data types

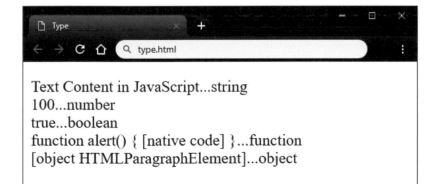

Text Content in JavaScript...string
100...number
true...boolean
function alert() { [native code] }...function
[object HTMLParagraphElement]...object

Don't get the same result? Check your code exactly matches the downloadable example source code – see page 6.

Notice how the + operator is used here to join parts of a string together, and the += operator adds strings onto existing strings.

79

Do arithmetic

The arithmetic operators that are most often used in JavaScript are listed in the table below with the operation they perform:

Operator:	Operation:
+	Add numbers or join strings together
–	Subtract
*	Multiply
/	Divide
%	Get the remainder after dividing
++	Increase by one
– –	Decrease by one

Values used with operators are called "operands". For example, in the statement **5 + 2** the **+** operator is given operand values of five and two.

Notice that the **+** operator performs two kinds of operation depending on the type of operands. Numeric operands are added to produce a sum total, but string operands are joined together to make a single string.

The **%** operator divides the first operand by the second operand and gets the remainder. Dividing by **2** will get either **1** or **0**. This can be used to tell if the first operand is an odd number or an even number.

The **++** operator and -- operator alter the value of a single operand by 1 and get the new value. These operators are mostly used to count up or down in a programming loop, and can be used in two different ways to different effect. When put in front of the operand its value gets immediately changed. When put after the operand its value gets changed after the operation.

Hot tip

The % remainder operator is also known as the "modulus" operator. The example on page 103 uses this operator to identify numbers as odd or even.

...cont'd

1 Create an HTML document that has an empty paragraph and a script element
```
<p id="msg" ></p>

<script>
// Code to replace this comment.
</script>
```

arithmetic.html

2 In the script element, write these lines of code to create and initialize variables by doing arithmetic
```
var sum = 80 + 20 ;    // Add two operands.
var sub = sum - 50 ;   // Subtract 2nd operand from 1st.
var mul = sum * 5 ;    // Multiply two operands.
var div = sum / 4 ;    // Divide 1st operand by 2nd.
var rem = sum % 2 ;    // Remainder after dividing by two.
var inc = ++sum ;      // Immediately increase by one.
var dec = --sum ;      // Immediately decrease by one.
```

3 Next, add these lines of code to join together strings and each variable value in a single string variable
```
var str = "Sum: " + sum + "<br>Subtracted: " + sub ;
str += "<br>Multiplied: " + mul ;
str += "<br>Divided: " + div + "<br>Remainder: " + rem ;
str += "<br>Increased: "  + inc ;
str += "<br>Decreased: " + dec ;
```

4 Now, add this statement to write the whole string into the paragraph
```
document.getElementById( "msg" ).innerHTML = str ;
```

5 Save the HTML document then open the web page in your browser to see the result of arithmetic

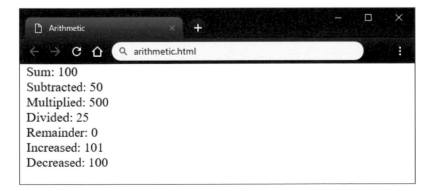

Move the ++ and -- operators behind the operands to see the difference – the result is
Increased: 100
Decreased: 101
Do you see why?
It's because the original values are now written in the paragraph before the variable values get changed.

Don't get the same result? Check your code exactly matches the downloadable example source code – see page 6.

Assign values

The operators that are used in JavaScript to assign values are listed in the table below. All except the simple = operator are a short version of a longer equivalent assignment:

Operator:	Example:	Equivalent To:
=	a = b	a = b
+=	a += b	a = (a + b)
–=	a –= b	a = (a – b)
*=	a *= b	a = (a * b)
/=	a /= b	a = (a / b)
%=	a %= b	a = (a % b)

Hot tip

The === Equality operator compares values and is fully explained on page 84.

It is important to think of the = operator as meaning "assign" rather than "equals" to avoid confusion with the === Equality operator, which is used to compare two values.

In the = example in the table above, the variable **a** gets assigned the value contained in variable **b** to become its new stored value.

The combined += operator is most useful and has been employed in previous examples to add a string onto an existing string.

When the variables contain numbers, the += example in the table will first add the value contained in variable **a** to that contained in variable **b**. It will then assign the sum total so that it becomes the new value stored in variable **a**.

All other combined assignment operators work in a similar way to the += operator. They each perform the arithmetic operation on their two operands first, then assign the result of that operation to the first variable so that it becomes its new stored value.

1 Create an HTML document that has an empty paragraph and a script element

```
<p id="msg" ></p>

<script>
// Code to replace this comment.
</script>
```

assign.html

2 In the script element, write these lines of code to initialize variables then assign each one a new value

```
var txt = "JS" ;   txt += " Fun" ;   // Join together.
var flt = 7.5 ;    flt += 2.25 ;     // Add and assign.
var sum = 8 ;      sum -= 4 ;        // Subtract and assign.
var mul = 24 ;     mul *= sum ;      // Multiply and assign.
var div = 24 ;     div /= sum ;      // Divide and assign.
var rem = 24 ;     rem %= sum ;      // Remainder and assign.
```

3 Next, add these lines of code to join together strings and each variable value in a single string variable

```
var str = "Add & assign string: "    + txt ;
str += "<br>Add & assign float: " + flt ;
str += "<br>Subtract & assign: "   + sum ;
str += "<br>Multiply & assign: "   + mul ;
str += "<br>Divide & assign: "       + div ;
str += "<br>Remainder & assign: " + rem ;
```

4 Now, add this statement to write the whole string into the paragraph

```
document.getElementById( "msg" ).innerHTML = str ;
```

5 Save the HTML document then open the web page in your browser to see the result of each operation

```
Assign              × +                    —  □  ×

←  →  C  ⌂    Q  assign.html                    ⋮

Add & assign string: JS Fun
Add & assign float: 9.75
Subtract & assign: 4
Multiply & assign: 96
Divide & assign: 6
Remainder & assign: 0
```

Don't get the same result? Check your code exactly matches the downloadable example source code – see page 6.

83

Compare values

The operators used in JavaScript to compare two values are listed in the table below:

Operator:	Comparison:
===	Equality
!==	Inequality
>	Greater Than
<	Less Than
>=	Greater Than or Equal
<=	Less Than or Equal

The === Equality operator compares two values and will return **true** if they are exactly equal, otherwise it will return **false**. If the values are identical numbers, they are equal. If the values are strings containing the same characters in the same positions, they are equal. If the values are Boolean values that are both **true**, or both **false**, they are equal.

The !== Inequality operator returns **true** if the two values are not equal, using the same rules as the === Equality operator.

Equality and Inequality operators are useful in comparing two values to perform "conditional branching", where the script will follow a particular direction according to the result returned.

The > Greater Than operator compares two values and returns **true** if the first value is greater than the second. The < Less Than operator makes the same comparison but returns **true** when the first value is less than the second. Adding the = character after the > Greater Than operator or the < Less Than operator makes them also return **true** when the two values are equal.

The > Greater Than and < Less Than operators are often used to test the value of a counter variable in a programming loop.

Hot tip

An example using the > Greater Than operator in a loop can be found on page 97.

84

...cont'd

1 Create an HTML document that has an empty paragraph and a script element

```
<p id="msg" ></p>

<script>
// Code to replace this comment.
</script>
```

compare.html

2 In the script element, write these lines of code to initialize a number of variables by comparing values

```
var result_1 = "JavaScript" === "JAVASCRIPT" ;
var result_2 = "JavaScript" === "JavaScript" ;
var result_3 = 7.5 === 7.5 ;       // Equality test.
var result_4 = 8 !== 8 ;           // Inequality test.
var result_5 = 24 > 12 ;           // Greater Than test.
var result_6 = 24 < 12 ;           // Less Than test.
var result_7 = 24 <= 24 ;          // Less Than or Equal test.
```

3 Next, add these lines of code to join together strings and each variable value in a single string variable

```
var str = "String Equality [test 1]: "     + result_1 ;
str += "<br>String Equality [test 2]: "     + result_2 ;
str += "<br>Float Equality test: "          + result_3 ;
str += "<br>Integer Inequality test: "      + result_4 ;
str += "<br>Greater Than test: "            + result_5 ;
str += "<br>Less Than test: "               + result_6 ;
str += "<br>Less Than or Equal test: "      + result_7 ;
```

4 Now, add this line to write the string into the paragraph

```
document.getElementById( "msg" ).innerHTML = str ;
```

5 Save the HTML document then open the web page in your browser to see the result of each comparison

```
 Compare               +           —  □  X
← → C ⌂  Q compare.html                    ⋮
String Equality [test 1]: false
String Equality [test 2]: true
Float Equality test: true
Integer Inequality test: false
Greater Than test: true
Less Than test: false
Less Than or Equal test: true
```

85

JavaScript is case-sensitive, so character capitalization must match for compared strings to be equal.

Don't get the same result? Check your code exactly matches the downloadable example source code – see page 6.

Assess logic

The three logical operators that can be used in JavaScript are listed in the table below:

Operator:	Operation:
&&	Logical AND
||	Logical OR
!	Logical NOT

The logical operators are used with operands that have a Boolean value of **true** or **false** – or values that can convert to **true** or **false**.

The **&&** logical AND operator will examine two values and return **true** only if both are **true**. Otherwise, the **&&** AND operator will return **false**. This is often used in "conditional branching" where the direction of the script is determined by testing two conditions. If both tests are successful then the script will follow a particular direction, otherwise it will follow a different direction.

Unlike the **&&** logical AND operator, which needs both values to be **true**, the **||** logical OR operator will examine two values and return **true** if either one of them is **true**. If neither one of the values is **true** then the **||** OR operator will return **false**. This is useful to have a script perform a certain action if either one of two tests are successful.

The third logical operator is the **!** logical NOT operator that is used before a single value to return the opposite of that value. For example, if variable **a** has a **true** value then **!a** would return **false**. This is useful to "toggle" the value of a variable on each pass of a programming loop. For example, the statement **a=!a** reverses the value on each pass – like flicking a light switch on and off.

1 Create an HTML document that has an empty paragraph and a script element

```
<p id="msg" ></p>

<script>
// Code to replace this comment.
</script>
```

logic.html

2 In the script element, write these lines of code to initialize a number of variables using each logic operator

```
var yes = true , no = false ;    // Initialize with booleans.
var result_1 = yes && yes ;      // Test if both are true.
var result_2 = yes && no ;       // Test if both are true.
var result_3 = no || yes ;       // Test if either is true.
var result_4 = no || no ;        // Test if either is true.
var result_5 = !yes ;            // Reverse the value.
```

3 Next, add these lines of code to join together strings and each variable value in a single string variable

```
var str = "Are both values true?: " + result_1 ;
str += "<br>Are both values true now?: " + result_2 ;
str += "<br>Is either value true?: " + result_3 ;
str += "<br>Is either value true now?: " + result_4 ;
str += "<br>Initial value: " + yes ;
str += "<br>Toggled value: " + result_5 ;
```

4 Now, add this line to write the string into the paragraph

```
document.getElementById( "msg" ).innerHTML = str ;
```

5 Save the HTML document then open the web page in your browser to see the result of each assessment

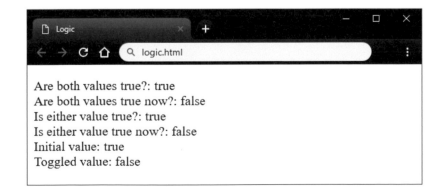

Don't get the same result? Check your code exactly matches the downloadable example source code – see page 6.

Force order

JavaScript operators have different levels of importance that decides the order in which a statement containing multiple different operators gets performed. The operations of operators with higher importance are performed before those of lower importance. The table below lists each type of operator in order of highest to lowest importance, from top to bottom in the table:

Operator:	Operation:	Importance:
* / %	Multiplication, Division, Remainder	Highest
+ –	Addition, Subtraction	
< <= > >=	Comparison	
=== !==	Equality Inequality	
&&	Logical AND	
||	Logical OR	
= += –= *= /= %=	Assignment	Lowest

It is important to understand the order in which operations are performed to avoid unwanted results from statements containing multiple operators. For example, look at this statement:

var sum = 9 + 12 / 3 ;

Here the division operation gets performed first, as the / division operator has higher importance than the + addition operator – so the result is **13** (12 / 3 = 4, 4 + 9 = 13).

You can force the order in which the operations get performed by enclosing an expression in ( ) round bracket "precedence operators" so that its operation will be performed first. In this example **(9 + 12) / 3** performs the addition first – so the result is now **7** (9 + 12 = 21, 21 / 3 = 7).

Hot tip

Make a habit of using ( ) round brackets to force the order in which operations get performed.

...cont'd

1 Create an HTML document that has an empty paragraph and a script element

```
<p id="msg" ></p>

<script>
// Code to replace this comment.
</script>
```

order.html

2 In the script element, write these lines of code to initialize two variables

```
var sum = 2 * 9 + 12 / 3 ;  // Equivalent to (2*9) + (12/3).
var str = "18 + 4 = " + sum ;
```

3 Next, add these lines of code to force operation order and join together strings in a single string variable

```
sum = ( (2 * 9 ) + 12 ) / 3 ;  // Equivalent to (18+12) / 3.
str += "<br>30 / 3 = " + sum ;

sum = ( 2 * ( 9 + 12 ) ) / 3 ;  // Equivalent to (2*21) / 3.
str += "<br>42 / 3 = " + sum ;

sum = 2 * ( 9 + ( 12 / 3 ) ) ;  // Equivalent to 2 * (9+4).
str += "<br>2 * 13 = " + sum ;
```

Operations enclosed in the innermost ( ) brackets get performed first.

89

4 Now, add this line to write the string into the paragraph

```
document.getElementById( "msg" ).innerHTML = str ;
```

5 Save the HTML document then open the web page in your browser to see the result of each operation

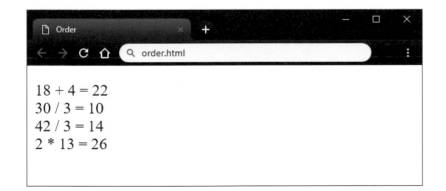

```
18 + 4 = 22
30 / 3 = 10
42 / 3 = 14
2 * 13 = 26
```

Don't get the same result? Check your code exactly matches the downloadable example source code – see page 6.

What you learned

● "JavaScript" is a programming language that can be used to provide functionality on a web page.

● The JavaScript keywords, reserved words, and object names must be avoided when choosing names in code.

● A script element can appear at the end of the body section of an HTML document between **<script>** and **</script>** tags.

● JavaScript single line comments begin with // and multi-line comments can be written between /* and */.

● JavaScript statements must end with a ; semicolon.

● Variables are created using the **var** keyword and can store any data type – boolean, number, string, function, or object.

● Arithmetic operators are **+** add, **–** subtract, ***** multiply, **/** divide, **%** remainder, **++** increase, and **– –** decrease.

● The **=** assignment operator should not be confused with the **===** equality operator that compares two values.

● Combined assignment operators **+=, –=, *=, /=** and **%=** each perform an arithmetic operation then assign its result.

● Comparison operators test for **===** equality, **!==** inequality, **>** greater, **>=** greater or equal, **<** less, **<=** less or equal.

● Logical **&&** AND returns **true** when both values are **true**, but logical **||** OR returns **true** when either value is **true**.

● Logical **!** NOT can be placed before a single value to return its opposite value.

● Operation order can be forced by enclosing an expression in **( )** round brackets to override the default order.

● Where a statement contains several expressions in **( )** round brackets, the innermost operation gets performed first.

7 Build Blocks of Code

Do something if

The progress of any computer program depends on the testing of conditions to decide the direction of flow. Each test may present one or more "branches" along which to continue according to the result of the test.

The basic conditional test in JavaScript is performed with an **if** keyword, which tests a condition for a Boolean **true** or **false** result.

When the result of a conditional test is **true** a statement following the test will be executed, otherwise that statement gets skipped and program flow continues at the next statement.

An **if** statement needs you to put the condition to be tested in **( )** round brackets after the **if** keyword, like this:

if (*condition*) *execute-this-statement-when-true* ;

An **if** statement can also have multiple statements to be executed when the result is **true** by enclosing the statements in **{ }** curly brackets to build a code block, like this:

```
if ( condition )
{
        execute-this-statement-when-true ;
        also-execute-this-statement-when-true ;
        also-execute-this-statement-when-true ;
}
```

Testing a condition and the execution of actions according to its result is just like your real-life thought process. For example, the actions you might execute on a summer day:

```
var temperature = readThermometer( ) ;
var tolerable = 25 ;

if ( temperature > tolerable )
{
        turnOnAircon( ) ;
        getCoolDrink( ) ;
        stayInShade( ) ;
}
```

This represents some of the actions to perform if the temperature is greater than 25 (degrees Celsius) on a summer day.

Hot tip

You can also enclose a single statement to be executed in curly brackets to maintain a consistent coding style.

...cont'd

1 Create an HTML document that has an empty paragraph and a script element
```
<p id="msg" ></p>

<script>

// Code to replace this comment.

</script>
```

if.html

2 In the script element, write these lines of code to initialize two variables and perform a conditional test of a value
```
var obj = document.getElementById( "msg" ) ;
var flag = true ;

if ( flag )
{
        obj.innerHTML = "Power is On" ;
}
```

This test is like writing **if(flag === true)** but you can leave out the **=== true** part, as the **if** keyword always tests for a **true** result.

3 Next, add two more conditional tests – one that will fail and one that will succeed
```
if ( 7 < 2 )
{
        obj.innerHTML += "<br>Failure" ;
}

if ( 7 > 2 )
{
        obj.innerHTML += "<br>Success" ;
}
```

4 Save the HTML document, then open it in your browser to see the content written only when tests succeed

```
If                    +              —  □  ×
←  →  C  ⌂   Q  if.html                    ⋮

Power is On
Success
```

Don't get the same result? Check your code exactly matches the downloadable example source code – see page 6.

Do something else

An **if** statement, which tests a condition for a Boolean result and only executes its statements when the result is **true**, provides a single branch that the script may follow. An alternative branch that the script can follow when the result is **false** can be provided by extending the **if** statement with the **else** keyword.

An **else** statement follows after the **if** statement, like this:

if (*condition*)   *execute-this-statement-when-true* ;

else   *execute-this-statement-when-false* ;

An **if-else** statement can also have multiple statements to be executed by enclosing statements in curly brackets, like this:

```
if ( condition )
{
        execute-this-statement-when-true ;
        also-execute-this-statement-when-true ;
}
else
{
        execute-this-statement-when-false ;
        also-execute-this-statement-when-false ;
}
```

Multiple branches can be provided by making more conditional **if** tests at the start of each **else** statement block, like this:

```
if ( condition )
{
        execute-these-statements-when-true ;
}
else if ( condition )
{
        execute-these-statements-when-true ;
}
else if ( condition )
{
        execute-these-statements-when-true ;
}
else
{
        execute-these-statements-when-false ;
}
```

An **if-else-if** statement might repeatedly test a variable for a range of values or might test a variety of conditions. The final **else** statement acts as a default for when no results return **true**.

Hot tip

When a test returns a **true** result in an **if-else** code block its associated statements get executed. Flow then continues after the **if-else** code block – without testing any more **else** statements in that block.

...cont'd

1 Create an HTML document that has an empty paragraph and a script element

```html
<p id="msg" ></p>

<script>
// Code to replace this comment.
</script>
```

else.html

2 In the script element, write these lines of code to initialize three variables with an object, a Boolean, and a number

```javascript
var obj = document.getElementById( "msg" ) ;
var flag = false ;
var num = 10 ;
```

3 Next, test the Boolean variable

```javascript
if ( flag )        obj.innerHTML = "Power is On" ;
else               obj.innerHTML = "Power is Off" ;
```

4 Now, test the value of the number

```javascript
if ( num === 5 )
{
        obj.innerHTML += "<br>Number is Five" ;
}
else if ( num === 10 )
{
        obj.innerHTML += "<br>Number is Ten" ;
}
else
{
        obj.innerHTML +="<br>Neither Five nor Ten" ;
}
```

5 Save the HTML document, then open it in your browser to see the content written only when tests succeed

Don't get the same result? Check your code exactly matches the downloadable example source code – see page 6.

Do something while

A programming loop is a code block that tests a condition and repeatedly executes one or more statements while the test result remains **true**.

Each test of the condition and execution of the statements in a loop is called a "pass". When the test result returns **false** no further passes are made and flow continues at the next statement following the loop code block.

The JavaScript **while** keyword begins a loop and needs you to put the condition to be tested in **( )** round brackets after the **while** keyword. This must be followed by statements to be executed inside **{ }** curly brackets to create a code block. Most importantly, the curly brackets must also contain a statement that, at some point during the loop, will change the result of the test to become **false** – otherwise you will create a never-ending loop!

```
while( condition )
{
        statements-to-be-executed ;
        statement-to-change-the-test-result ;
}
```

If the test result returns **false** on the very first pass, the loop exits immediately so the statements in its curly brackets are never executed.

A **while** loop can be made to perform a set number of passes by using a counter variable as the test condition and increasing its value on each pass. For example, a **while** loop code block to execute a set of statements 100 times, like this:

```
var i = 0 ;

while ( i < 100 )
{
        // Statements to be executed go here.
        i++ ;
}
```

The counter variable is increased by 1 on each pass until its value reaches 100. At that point the test result returns **false** and the loop ends.

Don't
forget

Every while loop must have curly brackets as they contain at least two statements – one statement to execute and one statement to change the test result.

...cont'd

1 Create an HTML document that has an empty paragraph and a script element

```
<p id="msg" ></p>

<script>
// Code to replace this comment.
</script>
```

while.html

2 In the script element, write these lines of code to initialize two variables with an object and a loop counter number

```
var obj = document.getElementById( "msg" ) ;
var num = 10 ;
```

3 Next, add a loop code block to write the counter number and decrease its value by 1 on each pass

```
while ( num > 0 )
{
        obj.innerHTML += num + "<br>" ;
        num-- ;
}
```

4 Now, add a statement to write content after the loop ends

```
obj.innerHTML += "LIFT OFF!" ;
```

Don't get the same result? Check your code exactly matches the downloadable example source code – see page 6.

5 Save the HTML document, then open it in your browser to see the countdown content written

```
[ While                    +          —  □  ✕
←  →  C  ⌂    Q  while.html              ⋮
10
9
8
7
6
5
4
3
2
1
LIFT OFF!
```

97

Loop through arrays

All the JavaScript variables you have seen in the previous examples have stored just one value, but variables can also store an "array" of many values. Array variables store values in separate "elements".

JavaScript arrays make much use of [ ] square bracket characters. You can create and initialize an array variable using them like this:

var *array-name* = [*value-1* , *value-2* , *value-3*] ;

The array elements are automatically numbered, starting at zero. So the first element is 0, the second is 1, the third is 2, and so on. This numbering system is called "zero-based indexing".

You get a value from an array by stating its element index number in [ ] square brackets following the array variable name. For example, **colors[0]** would get the value stored in the first element of an array named "colors".

If you don't want to initialize an array immediately, you can create an empty array then assign values to its elements later, like this:

var colors = [ ] ;   // Create an empty array.

colors[0] = "Red" ;   // Assign an element value.

colors[1] = "White" ;   // Assign an element value.

colors[2] = "Blue" ;   // Assign an element value.

Array variables have a useful **length** property that automatically stores a number, which is the number of elements in the array. For example, with the array above, **colors.length** would return **3**. Notice that the length number will always be one more than the final element's index number – because of zero-based indexing.

Arrays and loops make great partners! A loop can be used to fill the elements of an array with values. The elements of even very large arrays can be filled in this way – and with very little code.

Similarly, loops can be used to quickly read the values in each array element and perform some action appropriate to that value on each pass of the loop.

...cont'd

① Create an HTML document that has an empty paragraph and a script element

```
<p id="msg" ></p>

<script>
// Code to replace this comment.
</script>
```

array.html

② In the script element, write these lines of code to initialize variables with an object and a loop counter number

```
var obj = document.getElementById( "msg" ) ;
var num = 0 ;
```

③ Next, add a statement to create and initialize an array that will store a different month name in each element

```
var summer = [ "June" , "July" , "August" ] ;
```

④ Now, insert a loop to write the index number and value of each array element into the paragraph

```
while ( num < summer.length )
{
        obj.innerHTML +=
        num + ": " + summer[ num ] + "<br>" ;
        num++ ;
}
```

Don't forget

Remember to include a statement in the loop code block that will at some point make the test result return false. Here the counter gets increased on each pass.

⑤ Now, insert a statement to write one selected array element's value into the panel

```
obj.innerHTML += "Vacation month: " + summer[ 2 ] ;
```

⑥ Save the HTML document, then open it in your browser to see the array element numbers and values

Don't get the same result? Check your code exactly matches the downloadable example source code – see page 6.

Make a function

A JavaScript "function" is simply a named block of code that can be called to execute the statements it contains at any time. You have already seen the built-in **alert( )** function called in previous examples to open a pop-up dialog box.

More excitingly, you can make your own functions by writing function code blocks to execute statements you write.

A function code block begins with the JavaScript **function** keyword, followed by a space and a name of your choice, then a pair of **( )** round brackets.

As with other code blocks, the statements to be executed by a function are contained in a pair of **{ }** curly brackets – so a function block looks like this:

```
function function-name ( )
{
        statements-to-be-executed ;
}
```

Some script authors prefer to put the opening **{** curly bracket on the same line as the function name, but you can align them like the example above. Statements you add inside the block may also have curly brackets, such as **if-else** statement blocks, so keeping all the curly brackets aligned makes it easier to read the code:

```
function summerDay()
{
    var temperature = readThermometer( ) ;

    if ( temperature > 25 )
    {
            turnOnAircon( ) ;
            getCoolDrink( ) ;
            stayInShade( ) ;
    }
}
```

Hot tip

Notice here how a function can include a statement that calls another function.

Hot tip

Functions that respond to events are called "event handlers".

Often you will want to make a function to respond to an event that occurs on a web page – for example, to perform some action in response to the click event that occurs when the user clicks a button. To do this you can assign the function name, including **( )** round brackets, to the **onclick** attribute in the **<button>** tag.

1 Create an HTML document that has an empty paragraph and a script element

```
<p id="msg" ></p>

<script>
// Code to replace this comment.
</script>
```

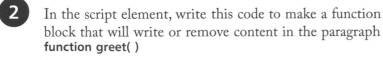

function.html

2 In the script element, write this code to make a function block that will write or remove content in the paragraph

```
function greet( )
{
        var obj = document.getElementById( "msg" ) ;

        if ( obj.innerHTML === "" )
        {
                obj.innerHTML = "Function says Hi!" ;
        }
        else
        {
                obj.innerHTML = "" ;
        }
}
```

Hot tip

An empty paragraph is seen here as an empty string in this test.

101

3 At the start of the body section of the document, add a button that will call the function when it gets clicked

```
<button onclick="greet( )" >Click Me</button>
```

4 Save the HTML document, then open it in your browser and click the button to see the function respond

Don't get the same result? Check your code exactly matches the downloadable example source code – see page 6.

Send in values

Perhaps you've been wondering why JavaScript function names are followed by a pair of ( ) round brackets? It's now time to find out...

The ( ) round brackets after the function name in a function code block let a value be sent to the function. They can enclose a "parameter" name of your choice. A parameter is like a variable – it can store a value sent from the caller, for use in the function statements. The function block now looks like this:

```
function function-name ( parameter-name )
{
        statements-to-be-executed ;
}
```

Parameter names must follow the same naming rules as those for variable and function names – they can include letters, numbers, and underscores, but can't include spaces or begin with a number.

A value is passed from the caller by putting the value in the ( ) round brackets after the function name in the function call. The value sent to the function is called the function "argument".

You have already seen a function argument in a previous example. With **onclick="alert('Start the Game')"** back on page 46 you passed a string argument to the built-in **alert( )** function.

Multiple parameters can be included in the ( ) round brackets of the function code block to let the caller pass multiple arguments. These parameters must be written as a comma-separated list:

```
function function-name ( param-1 , param-2 , param-3 )
{
        statements-to-be-executed ;
}
```

Hot tip

You can also assign a value to the parameter in the ( ) round brackets to be used as a default value if the caller does not send a value.

Similarly, the caller must put the values in the ( ) round brackets of the function call as a comma-separated list.

It is important to remember that the function call must normally pass the same number of argument values as there are parameters. They must be in the correct order too.

1 Create an HTML document that has an empty paragraph and a script element

```
<p id="msg" ></p>

<script>
// Code to replace this comment.
</script>
```

argument.html

2 In the script element, write this code to make a function block that will rate an argument value sent from the caller

```
function rate( num )
{
        var obj = document.getElementById( "msg" ) ;

        if ( num % 2 === 0 )
        {
                obj.innerHTML = num + " is Even" ;
        }
        else
        {
                obj.innerHTML = num + " is Odd" ;
        }
}
```

3 At the start of the body section of the document, add two buttons that each call the function when they get clicked

```
<button onclick="rate( 1 )" >One</button>
<button onclick="rate( 2 )" >Two</button>
```

4 Save the HTML document, then open it in your browser and click each button to send values to the function

Don't get the same result? Check your code exactly matches the downloadable example source code – see page 6.

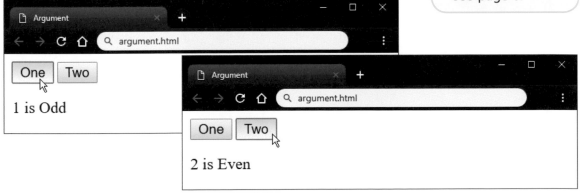

Return a value

The JavaScript functions that you have seen so far will execute their statements when called, and may be sent values by the caller. Functions can be made to also send a value back to the caller by adding a **return** statement in the function code block:

```
function function-name ( parameter/s )
{
        statements-to-be-executed ;

        return value-to-be-returned ;
}
```

The returned value may be the result of some operation performed on argument values sent to the function parameters. For example:

```
function multiply( a , b )
{
        return ( a * b ) ;          // e.g. multiply( 3, 2 ) returns 6.
}
```

Often the returned value from a "utility" function of this sort will be assigned to a variable for use in the calling function.

Utility functions can also be used for validation – to test argument values to see if they are what is expected. In this case the returned value will be Boolean **true** if valid, or Boolean **false** if invalid. There is a built-in **isNaN( )** function that tests for non-numeric values:

```
function isValidNumber( arg )
{
        if( isNaN( arg ) ) return false ;
}
```

A **return** statement can also be used to exit from a function if a condition has been met. For example, to end a game program after a number of tries have been made.

Now, a final word on functions – function statements can call other functions, but they can also call the function in which they appear. These are called "recursive" functions.

A recursive function acts like loop, executing the statements it contains on each pass. Likewise, a recursive function must perform a test that at some point will return a **false** result to exit. Usually a recursive function will change the value of an argument that it sends on each pass, and this is the value that will be tested.

Hot tip

The "is Not a Number" **isNaN( )** function returns **true** when its argument is non-numeric. When its argument is a string, for example, it's **true** that the argument is non-numeric.

...cont'd

1 Create an HTML document that has an empty paragraph and a script element

```
<p id="msg" ></p>

<script>
// Code to replace this comment.
</script>
```

return.html

2 In the script element, write this code to make a function block that will call itself repeatedly

```
function run( num )
{
        var obj = document.getElementById( "msg" ) ;

        if ( num > 4 )
        {
                obj.innerHTML += "<br>Game Over!" ;
                return true ;
        }
        else
        {
                obj.innerHTML += "<br>Try #" + num ;
                num++ ;
                run( num ) ;
        }
}
```

Remember to include a statement in the recursive function code block that will at some point make the test result become **false**. Here the argument value gets increased on each pass.

3 At the start of the body section of the document, add a button that calls the function when clicked

```
<button onclick="run( 1 )" >Go</button>
```

4 Save the HTML document, then open it in your browser and click the button to run the recursive function

```
Return                      +         —  □  ×

C ⌂   Q return.html                       :

Go

Try #1
Try #2
Try #3
Try #4
Game Over!
```

Don't get the same result? Check your code exactly matches the downloadable example source code – see page 6.

What you learned

- The **if** keyword tests a condition for a **true** or **false** result.

- A condition to be tested by an **if** statement must be placed in **( )** round brackets after the **if** keyword.

- The statements to be executed when an **if** statement result is **true** must be placed in **{ }** curly brackets to build a code block.

- The **else** keyword provides an alternative branch that the script can follow when an **if** statement result is **false**.

- Multiple branches can be provided by making more conditional **if** tests at the start of each **else** statement block.

- The **while** keyword tests a condition and repeatedly executes its statements in a loop – until the test result becomes **false**.

- The **{ }** curly brackets of a **while** loop must contain a statement that will change the result of the test to **false**.

- A **while** loop can increase a tested counter variable on each pass to perform a set number of passes.

- An array variable stores values in separate elements, which are automatically numbered – starting at zero.

- An array element is addressed by stating its index number in **[ ]** square brackets after the array variable name.

- A loop can be used to fill the elements of an array with values and quickly read the values in each array element.

- A function is a named block of code that can be called to execute the statements it contains in **{ }** curly brackets.

- A function block begins with the **function** keyword followed by a given name and a pair of **( )** round brackets.

- The **( )** round brackets in a function code block can include a list of parameters that allow values to be sent to the function.

- A function can send a value back to the caller by including a **return** statement in the function code block.

- Statements in a function block can call other functions, and a recursive function can call itself to perform like a loop.

8 Use Built-in Functions

This chapter shows you how to call built-in JS functions to interact with a web page.

Confirm options

JavaScript provides a number of standard built-in functions that you can call to interact with the user. In previous examples you have already seen how you can pass a string argument to the built-in **alert( )** function to display a message on a pop-up dialog.

The dialog displayed by the **alert( )** function only has an "OK" button. When the user clicks the OK button it simply closes the dialog box – the **alert( )** function <u>does not</u> return a value.

If you want to provide the user with yes/no options you can call the built-in **confirm( )** function. This also accepts a string argument that will be displayed on a pop-up dialog, so you can ask the user a question in the displayed message.

Unlike the dialog displayed by the **alert( )** function, the dialog displayed by the **confirm( )** function typically has an "OK" button and a "Cancel" button. When the user clicks either of these buttons it closes the dialog box. But unlike the **alert( )** function, the **confirm( )** function <u>does</u> return a value:

- **OK** returns a Boolean **true** value to the caller.

- **Cancel** returns a Boolean **false** value to the caller.

You can usefully assign the result returned by the **confirm( )** function to a variable. The result can then be tested by an **if-else** statement to decide how the program should proceed:

confirm.html

1 Create an HTML document that has an empty paragraph and a script element
<p id="msg" ></p>

<script>
// Code to replace this comment.
</script>

2 In the script element, write this code to make a function block that begins by initializing two variables
function ask( )
{
      var obj = document.getElementById("msg") ;
      var ok = confirm("Do you want to continue?") ;

      // More code to be added here.

}

...cont'd

3 Now, in the function block, add a conditional test to
display an appropriate response to the user
if(ok)
{   **obj.innerHTML = "<img src='smile.png' >" ;**
          obj.innerHTML += "Great, let's continue." ;
}
else
{
          obj.innerHTML = "<img src='frown.png' >" ;
          obj.innerHTML += "Sorry to see you leave." ;
}

smile.png
(48px x 48px)

frown.png
(48px x 48px)

4 At the start of the body section of the document, add a
button that will call the function when it gets clicked
<button onclick="ask( )" >Ask the User</button>

5 Save the HTML document, then open it in your browser
and click the buttons to see appropriate responses

> **Don't get the same
> result?** Check your
> code exactly matches
> the downloadable
> example source code
> – see page 6.

Prompt for input

JavaScript provides a built-in **prompt( )** function to display a message on a pop-up dialog requesting user input.

The dialog displayed by the **prompt( )** function has a text input box. It also typically has an "OK" button and a "Cancel" button. When the user clicks either of these buttons it closes the dialog box. But unlike the **alert( )** function, the **prompt( )** function does return a value:

- **OK** returns a string value to the caller.

- **Cancel** returns a special **null** value to the caller.

The **prompt( )** function accepts a string argument that will be displayed on a pop-up dialog – so you can ask for input in the displayed message. It also accepts an optional second argument that will appear in the text input box. Whatever value is in that box will be returned when the user clicks the OK button.

The JavaScript **null** keyword represents a value of absolutely nothing – not even an empty string or zero.

You can usefully assign the result returned by the **prompt( )** function to a variable. The result can then be tested by an **if-else** statement to decide how the program should proceed:

prompt.html

1 Create an HTML document that has an empty paragraph and a script element
```
<p id="msg" ></p>

<script>
// Code to replace this comment.
</script>
```

2 In the script element, write this code to make a function block that begins by initializing a variable
```
function ask( )
{
        var obj = document.getElementById( "msg" ) ;

        // More code to be added here.
}
```

3 Now, in the function block, add a statement to request user input, and provide a default name value
```
var user = prompt( "Please enter your name", "User" ) ;
```

4 Next, in the function block, add a statement to request user input without providing a default value
var fav = prompt("What's your favorite color " + user) ;

5 Finally, in the function block, add a conditional test to exit if the user clicks Cancel or to display the user input
```
if( fav === null )
{
        return true ;
}
else if ( fav !== "" )
{
        obj.innerHTML = user + "'s favorite is " + fav ;
}
else
{
        obj.innerHTML = user + " has no favorite color" ;
}
```

Hot tip

If the user simply clicks OK on each prompt dialog, the message will read "User" (the default) " has no favorite color".

6 At the start of the body section of the document, add a button that will call the function when it gets clicked
<button onclick="ask( )" >Ask the User</button>

Don't get the same result? Check your code exactly matches the downloadable example source code – see page 6.

7 Save the HTML document, then open it in your browser and click the buttons to see the user input displayed

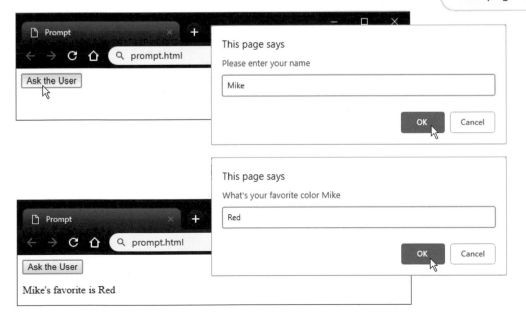

111

Get dates

JavaScript provides a built-in **Date** object that you can use to handle dates in your code. You first have to make a new copy of this object using the JavaScript **new** keyword, like this:

var *date-name* = new Date( ) ;

A new **Date** object initially stores date and time details of the time at which it was created. It also provides the "get" and "set" methods (functions) listed in the table below, which you can use to get or change each part of the stored date and time:

Hot tip

Functions provided by an object are more properly called "methods".

Get Methods:	Set Methods:
date-name.getFullYear( )	*date-name*.setFullYear( )
date-name.getMonth( )	*date-name*.setMonth( )
date-name.getDate( )	*date-name*.setDate( )
date-name.getDay( )	*date-name*.setDay( )
date-name.getHours( )	*date-name*.setHours( )
date-name.getMinutes( )	*date-name*.setMinutes( )
date-name.getSeconds( )	*date-name*.setSeconds( )

The **getMonth( )** and **getDay( )** methods only return an index number for the month (0-11, starting at January) and the day (0-6, starting at Sunday). This means you need to make an array of the month and day names, then use the index number returned by these methods to get the associated names:

date.html

1 Create an HTML document that has an empty paragraph and a script element
<p id="msg" ></p>

<script>
// Code to replace this comment.
</script>

2 In the script element, write this code to create and initialize two variables to each store an object

```
var obj = document.getElementById( "msg" ) ;
var now = new Date( ) ;
```

3 Set the year, then display the whole **Date** object

```
now.setFullYear( 2021 ) ;
obj.innerHTML = now ;
```

4 Create and initialize arrays of short day and month names

```
var days =
  [ "Sun", "Mon", "Tue", "Wed", "Thu", "Fri", "Sat" ] ;
var months = [ "Jan", "Feb", "Mar", "Apr", "May",
        "Jun", "Jul", "Aug", "Sep", "Oct", "Nov", "Dec" ] ;
```

5 Create and initialize variables to store separate parts of the **Date** object

```
var day = days[ now.getDay( ) ] ;
var mm = months[ now.getMonth( ) ] ;
var dd  = now.getDate( ) ;
var hrs = now.getHours( ) ;
var min = now.getMinutes( ) ;
if( min < 10 ) { min = "0" + min ; }
```

6 Next, display the stored date

```
obj.innerHTML += "<br>Date: "+day+", "+mm+" "+dd ;
```

7 Now, display the stored time

```
obj.innerHTML += "<br>Time: " + hrs + ":" + min ;
```

8 Save the HTML document, then open it in your browser and click the buttons to see the date and time

Wed Nov 10 2021 10:16:23 GMT+0200
                          (Eastern European Standard Time)

Date: Wed, Nov 10
Time: 10:16

Hot tip

Include this line to display a leading zero for single minutes – so that 10:5 becomes 10:05.

113

Hot tip

Notice that the final part of the **Date** object stores the local timezone offset. You can get this part from the object with a **getTimezoneOffset( )** method to see the number of minutes it is offset from GMT.

Don't get the same result? Check your code exactly matches the downloadable example source code – see page 6.

Convert values

You may sometimes need to convert values in your script to a different data type so an operation can be performed correctly. For example, if you prompt the user for a number it may be seen as a string version of the number, so arithmetic will not work.

JavaScript provides a useful built-in function called **parseInt( )** that examines a string argument in its **( )** round brackets, then returns a whole (integer) number copied from the start of the string – if that is possible.

There is also a function called **parseFloat( )** that examines a string argument in its **( )** round brackets, and returns a decimal (floating-point) number copied from the start of the string – if possible.

Where **parseInt( )** or **parseFloat( )** do not find a number at the start of a string they return a special **NaN** (Not a Number) value.

You can test if a value is not a number with the built-in **isNaN( )** function. This function returns **true** if its argument is a string – even if it's an empty string.

If you want to convert a number to a string you can tack the built-in **toString( )** function onto the name of the variable containing the string. This will return the number as a string – but will not convert the data type of the stored number to a string.

To convert a number stored in a variable you have to assign the string version to the variable to change its data type.

Hot tip

You saw the **isNaN( )** function in the example back on page 104.

HTML

convert.html

1 Create an HTML document that has an empty paragraph and a script element
<p id="msg" ></p>

<script>
// Code to replace this comment.
</script>

2 In the script element, write this code to create and initialize variables to store an object and user input
var obj = document.getElementById("msg") ;
var num = prompt("Please Enter a Number") ;

...cont'd

3 Next, display the type of user input and try to perform arithmetic on that value

```
obj.innerHTML = num + " [" + typeof num + "]<br>" ;
obj.innerHTML += num + "+2=" +( num + 2 )+ "<hr>";
```

4 Now, try to convert the user input to a number data type

```
num = parseFloat( num ) ;
```

5 Make a test to exit if the input is not a number, or attempt arithmetic then convert the number to a string

```
if( isNaN( num ) )
{
        obj.innerHTML += "Not a Number!" ;

}
else
{
  obj.innerHTML +=  num +" ["+ typeof num + "]<br>";
  obj.innerHTML += num + "+2="+( num + 2 )+"<hr>";

  num = num.toString( ) ;
  obj.innerHTML +=  num +" ["+ typeof num + "]" ;
}
```

6 Save the HTML document, then open it in your browser and enter input to convert values

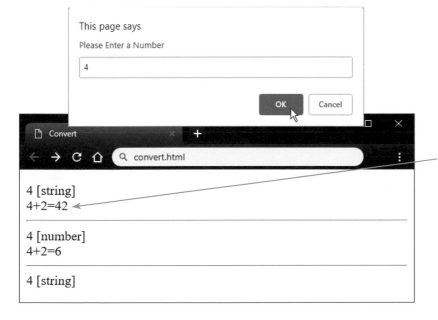

Beware

If you do not convert the string value to a number before arithmetic the two values get joined into a single "42" string.

> **Don't get the same result?** Check your code exactly matches the downloadable example source code – see page 6.

Round numbers

JavaScript provides a built-in **Math** object that has useful methods (functions) that you can use to work with numbers:

● The **Math.round( )** method rounds a number argument up or down to the closest whole number.

● The **Math.floor( )** method rounds down to the closest whole number below its argument value.

● The **Math.ceil( )** method rounds up to the closest whole number above its argument value.

round.html

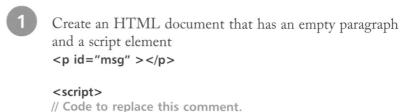

1 Create an HTML document that has an empty paragraph and a script element
```
<p id="msg" ></p>

<script>
// Code to replace this comment.
</script>
```

2 In the script element, write this code to create and initialize variables to store an object and a decimal number
```
var obj = document.getElementById( "msg" ) ;
var num =7.25 ;
```

3 Add statements to display the number and rounded values
```
obj.innerHTML = "Number: " + num + "<hr>" ;
obj.innerHTML +=  "Round: " + Math.round( num ) ;
obj.innerHTML += "<br>Floor: " + Math.floor( num ) ;
obj.innerHTML += "<br>Ceiling: " + Math.ceil( num ) ;
```

4 Save the HTML document, then open it in your browser to see the rounded numbers

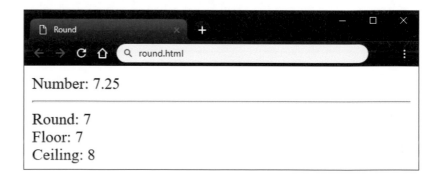

...cont'd

The JavaScript built-in **Math** object also has useful methods to compare numbers to find the greater and lesser value:

- The **Math.max( )** method needs two number arguments and will return the greater number.

- The **Math.min( )** method needs two number arguments and will return the lesser number.

1 Create an HTML document that has an empty paragraph and a script element

```
<p id="msg" ></p>

<script>
// Code to replace this comment.
</script>
```

maxmin.html

2 In the script element, write this code to create and initialize variables to store an object and two numbers

```
var obj = document.getElementById( "msg" ) ;
var dozen = 12 ;
var score = 20 ;
```

3 Add statements to display the numbers, plus the greater and lesser values

```
obj.innerHTML = "Numbers: " + dozen + " , " + score ;
obj.innerHTML +=
        "<hr>Maximum: " + Math.max( dozen, score ) ;
obj.innerHTML +=
        "<br>Minimum: " + Math.min( dozen, score ) ;
```

4 Save the HTML document, then open it in your browser and enter input to see the maximum and minimum values

```
MaxMin                                    +
←  →  C  ⌂   🔍 maxmin.html                    ⋮

Numbers: 12 , 20
_____

Maximum: 20
Minimum: 12
```

Don't get the same result? Check your code exactly matches the downloadable example source code – see page 6.

Random numbers

The JavaScript **Math.random( )** method returns a random floating-point number between 0.0 and, up to but not including, 1.0. This can be used for a variety of web page effects such as random banner rotation or random lottery number selection.

Multiplying the random floating-point value will increase its range. For example, multiplying it by 10 increases the range to between 0.0 and, up to but not including, 10.0.

Generally it is useful to round the random value up with the **Math.ceil( )** method so that the range becomes 1 to 10.

The process to get a random number can be written as separate steps, or **( )** round brackets can be used to get a random number with a single statement. For example, setting a range of 1 to 10 for a variable named "rand" can be written like this:

```
var rand = Math.random( ) ;
rand = rand * 10 ;
rand = Math.ceil( rand ) ;
```

or it can be written, more compactly, like this:

```
var rand = Math.ceil( Math.random( ) * 10 ) ;
```

random.html

1 Create an HTML document that has an empty paragraph and a script element
```
<p id="msg" ></p>

<script>
// Code to replace this comment.
</script>
```

2 In the script element, write this code to create and initialize a variable to store an object
```
var obj = document.getElementById( "msg" ) ;
```

3 Next, create several empty variables
```
var counter = 1 ;        // A loop counter.
var rand ;               // Random number store.
var temp ;               // Temporary number store.
var str ;                // Output string store.
var nums = [ ] ;         // Array of numbers store.
```

4 Now, fill array elements 1 to 59 with their index number

```
while ( counter < 60 )
{
        nums[ counter ] = counter ;
        counter++ ;
}
```

5 Then, mix up the numbers in the elements

```
counter = 1 ;
while ( counter < 60 )
{
        rand = Math.ceil( Math.random( ) * 59 ) ;
        temp = nums[ counter ] ;
        nums[ counter ] = nums[ rand ] ;
        nums[ rand ] = temp ;
        counter++ ;
}
```

Hot tip

Step 5 is a sorting algorithm that makes sure no two elements store the same number.

6 Finally, write a string including the numbers from array elements 1 to 6

```
counter = 1 ;
str = "Your Six Lucky Numbers: " ;
while ( counter < 7 )
{
        str += nums[ counter ] + " " ;
        counter++ ;
}
obj.innerHTML = str ;
```

Don't get the same result? Check your code exactly matches the downloadable example source code – see page 6.

7 Save the HTML document, then open it in your browser to see six random numbers each time you open the page

Your Six Lucky Numbers: 51 6 12 1 50 14

Your Six Lucky Numbers: 30 33 10 13 59 15

Here the random numbers are in the range 1 to 59 – to play the UK Lotto game or the US New York Lotto game.

119

Make a timer

JavaScript has a built-in **setTimeout( )** method that can test a condition or call a function after a delay of a set period of time. This method needs two arguments in its **( )** round brackets – the test condition or function to call, and the delay time:

setTimeout(*test-condition-or-function-to-call* , *delay-time*) ;

The amount of time to delay must be given in milliseconds, where 1000 is one second, 2000 is two seconds, and so on.

The **setTimeout( )** method returns a value that can be assigned to a variable to store the timer, like this:

var *timer-name* = setTimeout(*test-or-function* , *delay-time*) ;

The stored timer value can then be given as the argument to a **clearTimeout( )** method to cancel the timer, like this:

clearTimeout(*timer-name*) ;

When the **setTimeout( )** method calls the function in which it appears, a recursive loop is created. This means that the function will be repeatedly executed after the set amount of time.

The loop can be stopped by calling the **clearTimeout( )** method to end the repeated execution of the function:

timer.html

1 Create an HTML document that has two buttons, an empty paragraph, and a script element
```
<button onclick="launch( )" >Count Down</button>
<button onclick="abort( )" >Abort Launch</button>

<p id="msg" ></p>

<script>
// Code to replace this comment.
</script>
```

2 In the script element, write this code to create and initialize a variable to store an object, a counter variable, and a variable to store a timer
```
var obj = document.getElementById( "msg" ) ;
var counter = 10 ;
var timer = 0 ;
```

...cont'd

3 Next, add an event-handler function that will repeatedly
execute after a one-second delay

```
function launch( )
{
        if( counter < 1 )
        {
                obj.innerHTML += "LIFT OFF!<hr>" ;
                counter = 10 ;
        }
        else
        {
                obj.innerHTML += counter + " - ";
                counter-- ;
                timer = setTimeout( launch , 1000 ) ;
        }
}
```

You must not include
round brackets after the
function name here.

4 Now, add an event-handler function that will cancel
repeated execution of the timer function

```
function abort( )
{
        obj.innerHTML += "ABORTED!<hr>" ;
        counter = 10 ;
        clearTimeout( timer ) ;
}
```

**Don't get the same
result?** Check your
code exactly matches
the downloadable
example source code
– see page 6.

5 Save the HTML document, then open it in your browser
and click the buttons to start and stop the timer function

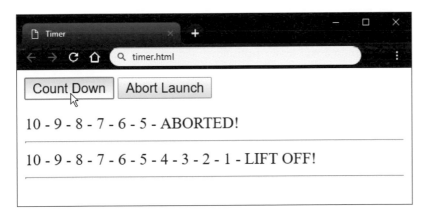

What you learned

- Then **alert( )** function does not return a value when the user clicks the OK button on its dialog box.

- The **confirm( )** function returns **true** when its OK button is clicked, and it returns **false** when its Cancel button is clicked.

- The **prompt( )** function returns a string when its OK button is clicked, and it returns **null** when its Cancel button is clicked.

- The result returned by the **confirm( )** and **prompt( )** functions can be tested by an **if-else** statement to decide how to proceed.

- The **Date** object has get and set methods to get or change each part of a stored date and time.

- The **new** keyword makes a copy of the built-in **Date** object.

- The **getMonth( )** and **getDay( )** methods return an index number that can get month and day names from arrays.

- The **parseInt( )** and **parseFloat( )** functions return a number from the start of a string or a **NaN** (Not a Number) value.

- The **toString( )** function converts a number to a string.

- The **Math.round( )**, **Math.floor( )**, and **Math.ceil( )** methods round their argument value to the closest whole number.

- The **Math.max( )** method needs two number arguments and will return the greater number.

- The **Math.min( )** method needs two number arguments and will return the lesser number.

- The **Math.random( )** method returns a random floating-point number between 0.0 and, up to but not including, 1.0.

- Multiplying a random floating-point value will increase its range and can be rounded up with the **Math.ceil( )** method.

- The **setTimeout( )** method that can test a condition or call a function after a delay of a set period of time.

- The **clearTimeout( )** method can be used to end the repeated execution of a timer function.

9 Grab Web Page Objects

Meet the DOM

When you open a web page in your browser it builds a family tree of its items. This tree is called the DOM – short for **D**ocument **O**bject **M**odel. Each item appears below the top-level **window** object, and the tree typically contains the branches shown below:

Items followed by **[ ]** square brackets are array objects, and those within **( )** round brackets are all the different possible types of form elements. Although the examples in this book do not use form elements it is useful to understand that they are a part of the DOM.

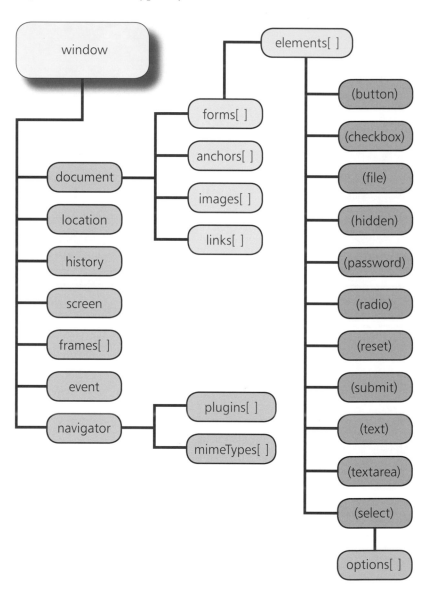

A special **for-in** loop can be used to list all properties of any object. This can be used to list all items of the **window.document** object to discover some of the DOM's tree features.

...cont'd

1 Create an HTML document that has an empty ordered list and a script element

```
<ol id="properties" ></ol>

<script>
// Code to replace this comment.
</script>
```

dom.html

2 In the script element, write this code to initialize two variables, to store an object and a property item

```
var obj = document.getElementById( "properties" ) ;
var item = null ;
```

3 Next, add a loop to list all properties and methods of the document

```
for ( item in window.document )
{
        obj.innerHTML += "<li>" + item + "</li>" ;
}
```

4 Save the HTML document, then open it in your browser to see all the document properties and methods

5 Scroll down the list, then use the browser's Find facility to find the **document.getElementById( )** method in the list – in Google Chrome press **Ctrl + F** keys to open Find

> **Don't get the same result?** Check your code exactly matches the downloadable example source code – see page 6.

125

```
DOM                                    —  □  X
←  →  C  ⌂   Q  dom.html                    ⋮
177. createElement      getElementById    1/1   ∧  ∨  ✕
178. createElementNS
179. caretRangeFromPoint
180. getSelection
181. elementFromPoint
182. elementsFromPoint
183. getElementById
184. prepend
185. append
186. querySelector
187. querySelectorAll
188. webkitCancelFullScreen
189. webkitExitFullscreen
190. createExpression
191. createNSResolver
192. evaluate
193. wasDiscarded
```

Don't forget

The property items are provided by the web browser so will vary by browser and version.

Grab one element

The DOM's **window.document** object can be written in your code simply as **document** – the top-level **window** object can be omitted.

The DOM's **document** object provides three useful methods that let you grab a reference to elements within the HTML document. You have already seen the first of these methods in previous examples, when grabbing a reference to an object using its **id** attribute value with the **document.getElementById( )** method.

A reference to an element in your JavaScript code lets you get and set values of that element. For example, you can change its colors with the **style.background** and **style.color** properties:

get-id.html

1 Create an HTML document that has a heading, a button, a paragraph element, and a script element
```
<h1 id="banr" >Web Page Banner</h1>

<button onclick="colorBanner( )" >
                Color the Banner</button>
<p id="para" >Background: None</p>

<script>
// Code to replace this comment.
</script>
```

2 In the script element, write this code to initialize three variables that grab a reference to two elements and specify an initial Boolean value
```
var banr = document.getElementById( "banr" ) ;
var para = document.getElementById( "para" ) ;
var flag = false ;
```

3 Next, add a function to reverse the Boolean value stored in the variable each time the function gets called
```
function colorBanner( )
{
        flag=!flag ;

        // Conditional test to replace this comment.

        // Statement to replace this comment.

}
```

...cont'd

4 Now, insert a conditional test to change element colors according to the current Boolean value of the variable

```
if( flag )
{
        banr.style.background="red" ;
        banr.style.color="white" ;
}
else
{
        banr.style.background="yellow" ;
        banr.style.color="blue" ;
}
```

The test is shorthand for the full test expression of **if(flag === true)**.

5 Add a statement to grab the current background state
`para.innerText="Background: " + banr.style.background ;`

6 Save the HTML document, then open it in your browser and click the button to change the element features

Don't get the same result? Check your code exactly matches the downloadable example source code – see page 6.

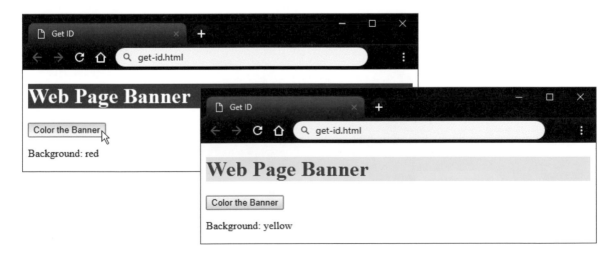

Grab many elements

In addition to the **document.getElementById( )** method, the **document** object provides a second method that lets you grab a reference to elements within the HTML document:

● The **document.getElementsByTagName( )** method – gets an array of all elements of the tag name given as its argument.

get-tags.html

1 Create an HTML document that has a table element and a script element
```
<table style="border:5px solid silver" > <tr>
<td>Apple</td>
<td>Banana</td>
<td>Cherry</td>
<td><button onclick="go( )" >Color</button> </td>
</tr> </table>

<script>
// Code to replace this comment.
</script>
```

2 In the script element, write this code to initialize two variables – to grab table data elements and set a counter
```
var cells = document.getElementsByTagName( "td" ) ;
var counter = 0 ;
```

3 Next, add a function to specify element properties
```
function go( )
{
    while( counter < cells.length )
    {
        cells[ counter ].style.background = "yellow" ;
        counter++ ;
    }
}
```

4 Save the HTML document, then open it in your browser and click the button to color some elements

...cont'd

Besides **document.getElementById( )** and **getElementsByTagName( )** methods, the **document** object provides a third method that lets you grab a reference to elements within the HTML document:

● The **document.getElementsByClassName( )** method – gets an array of all elements of the class name given as its argument.

1 Create an HTML document that has a table element and a script element

```
<table style="border:5px solid silver" > <tr>
<td class="hi" >Apple</td> <td>Banana</td>
<td class="hi" >Cherry</td>
<td> <button onclick="go( )" >Color</button> </td>
</tr> </table>

<script>
// Code to replace this comment.
</script>
```

get-class.html

2 In the script element, write this code to initialize two variables – to grab class elements and set a counter

```
var hilite = document.getElementsByClassName( "hi" ) ;
var counter = 0 ;
```

3 Next, add a function to specify element properties

```
function go( )
{
    while( counter < hilite.length )
    {
        hilite[ counter ].style.background = "red" ;
        hilite[ counter ].style.color = "white" ;
        counter++ ;
    }
}
```

Don't get the same result? Check your code exactly matches the downloadable example source code – see page 6.

4 Save the HTML document, then open it in your browser and click the button to color some elements

Set event listeners

Just as you can separate document presentation from structure by replacing HTML tag **style** attributes with style sheet rules, you can separate function from structure by replacing HTML tag event attributes (such as **onclick**) with script "event listeners".

Once you have an object reference to an element you can add an **addEventListener( )** method to the object to have it respond to user actions. This method needs two arguments in its **( )** round brackets – to state the type of event it should listen out for, and the name of a function to call in response when that event occurs.

The event name to listen for must be in quote marks. For example, replacing the **onclick** attribute by listening for the **"click"** event:

obj.**addEventListener("click" ,** *function-name* **) ;**

The function name does not need trailing **( )** brackets, but if the response is only a single line of code you can write an "anonymous function" (that has no name) as the second argument, like this:

obj.**addEventListener("event-name" ,**
                            function( ) { *statement-to-execute* **; }) ;**

Multiple event listeners can be added to an element to respond to different events created by user actions:

listen.html

1 Create an HTML document that has a heading, a button, a table, and a script element

```
<h1 id="banr" >Web Page Banner</h1>
<button id="btn" >Color the Banner</button>
<table> <tr>
<td class="cell" >Cell 1</td>
<td class="cell" >Cell 2</td>
<td class="cell" >Cell 3</td>
</tr> </table>

<script>
// Code to replace this comment.
</script>
```

2 In the document's head section, add a style sheet to set the table's presentation

```
<style>
table    { width:360px; height:120px;
              border:5px solid silver; text-align:center }
</style>
```

3 In the script element, write this code to initialize three variables that grab a reference to several elements

```
var banr = document.getElementById( "banr" ) ;
var btn = document.getElementById( "btn" ) ;
var cells = document.getElementsByClassName( "cell" ) ;
```

4 Next, add a statement that listens for click events, and a function to respond when they occur

```
btn.addEventListener( "click", colorBanner ) ;

function colorBanner( )
{
        banr.style.background="red" ;
        banr.style.color="white" ;
}
```

5 Now, add a loop that listens for mouse events, and calls anonymous functions to respond when they occur

```
var i=0 ;
while( i < cells.length )
{
   cells[ i ].addEventListener( "mouseover",
        function( ) { this.style.background="yellow" ; } ) ;
   cells[ i ].addEventListener( "mouseout",
        function( ) { this.style.background="none" ; } ) ;
   i++ ;
}
```

Hot tip

The variable name "i" is often used for a simple counter variable.

131

6 Save the HTML document, then open it in your browser and use the mouse to color some elements

Don't get the same result? Check your code exactly matches the downloadable example source code – see page 6.

Grab element text

You can copy text from an HTML element to examine the content in your script code. This might be used for simple validation against what you expect the content to contain.

JavaScript has a useful **indexOf( )** method that needs a string argument, in its **( )** round brackets, and will return a positive integer when the content contains that string. This might be used in a function to see if an email address looks to be a valid format.

A function can be called after the web page has loaded by setting the function name to the DOM's **window.onload** property:

content.html

1. Create an HTML document that has two empty paragraph elements, and one script element
```
<p id="adr" ></p>
<p id="msg" ></p>

<script>
// Code to replace this comment.
</script>
```

2. In the script element, write this code to initialize two variables that each grab a reference to a paragraph
```
var adr = document.getElementById( "adr" ) ;
var msg = document.getElementById( "msg" ) ;
```

3. Next, add a function to check an email address format, and to call a function after two seconds if the check fails
```
function checkAddress( )
{
        var str = adr.innerText ;
        if( str.indexOf( "@" ) === -1 )
        {
                msg.innerText="Email Address has no @" ;
                setTimeout( getAddress , 2000 ) ;
        }
        else if( str.indexOf( "." ) === -1 )
        {
                msg.innerText="Email Address has no ." ;
                setTimeout( getAddress , 2000 ) ;
        }
        else
        {
                msg.innerText="Email Address is Valid" ;
        }
}
```

The **indexOf( )** method returns a number that is the first character's position in the string when its argument value is found, or -1 when its argument value is not found in the string.

...cont'd

4 Now, add a function to request the user enters an email address, and calls the function to check their entry

```
function getAddress( )
{
        adr.innerText=prompt( "Enter Email Address" ) ;
        checkAddress( ) ;
}
```

5 Finally, add a statement to request the email address when the web page first loads

```
onload=getAddress ;
```

The top-level **window** object can be omitted from your code, so **window.onload** can be written more simply as **onload** in your code.

6 Save the HTML document, then open it in your browser and enter an email address for validation

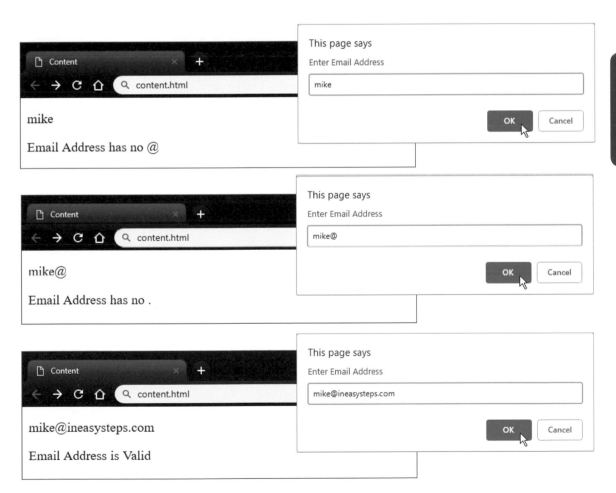

133

Manage taps and clicks

Touchscreen devices, such as smartphones, recognize "touch" events that occur when the user touches the screen. You can make your code respond to these events by adding an event listener – just like you do to respond to "click" events.

A tap action is like a mouse click, and mobile browsers typically convert a tap action to fire a "click" event after 300 milliseconds. This delay lets the browser see if the user performs a further touch action so it can be sure that it really should fire a "click" event. Unfortunately this delay can make your web page seem slow, so it is far better to have your code listen for a "touchend" event that occurs in touchscreen devices after the user taps an object.

It isn't enough to only listen for "touchend" events though, as you will still want your web page to respond in desktop browsers. This means that your code should listen for both "click" and "touchend" events to be universally responsive.

Listening for both "click" and "touchend" events creates a problem in touchscreen devices as both events are recognized by the mobile web browser – a touch event is fired after a tap action, then an additional click event is fired 300 milliseconds later. This means that your event handler function will get called twice!

The solution to this problem is to call the **preventDefault( )** method of the event to disable the web browser's usual behavior. This stops the default response to the "click" and "touchend" events so your own event handler code can respond:

touch.html

1 Create an HTML document that has a paragraph, containing a button and text, and a script element
```
<p>
<button id="startButton" >Start</button>
Hits: <strong id="scoreBoard" >0</strong>
</p>

<script>
// Code to replace this comment.
</script>
```

2 In the script element, write this code to initialize two variables that grab a reference to two elements
```
var start = document.getElementById( "startButton" ) ;
var board = document.getElementById( "scoreBoard" ) ;
```

...cont'd

3 Next, add statements that listen for click and touchend
events and call a function to respond when they occur
start.addEventListener("click" , tapOrClick) ;
start.addEventListener("touchend" , tapOrClick) ;

4 Now, add the function to prevent default behavior but
respond when either event occurs
function tapOrClick(event)
{
       event.preventDefault( ) ;
       board.innerText = parseInt(board.innerText) + 1 ;
       return false ;
}

Notice that the event is
passed as an argument
to the event handler
function, and the
function returns **false** to
end its execution.

5 Save the HTML document, then open it in your web
desktop browser and click the button to increase the hit
counter by 1 upon each click event

**Don't get the same
result?** Check your
code exactly matches
the downloadable
example source code
– see page 6.

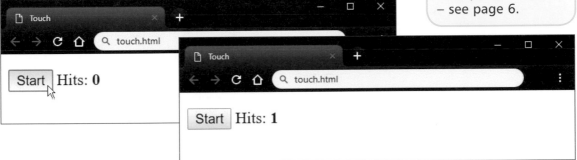

6 Open the
HTML
document in
a mobile web
browser and
tap the button
to increase the
hit counter by
1 upon each
touchend event

Set element state

Once you have a reference to elements in your JavaScript code you can set values to dynamically alter the state of their features:

● Set element background color with **style.background**

● Set element foreground color with **style.color**

● Set element visibility state with **style.visibility**

● Set element enabled/disabled state with **.disabled**

● Set element content with **.innerText** or **.innerHTML**

state.html

1 Create an HTML document that has a table element and a script element
```
<table  style="width:360px;height:50px" > <tr>
<td>
<button id="startButton" onclick="startGame( )" >
        Start</button>Hits: <b id="scoreBoard" >0</b>
</td>
<td id="clickPanel" onclick="addScore( )" >Click</td>
</tr> </table>

<script>
// Code to replace this comment.
</script>
```

2 In the script element, write this code to initialize three variables that will each store a reference to an element
```
var start = document.getElementById( "startButton" ) ;
var board = document.getElementById( "scoreBoard" ) ;
var panel = document.getElementById( "clickPanel" ) ;
```

3 Next, add a statement to set an initial element state
```
panel.style.visibility = "hidden" ;
```

4 Now, add a function to specify other element properties
```
function startGame( )
{
        panel.style.visibility = "visible" ;
        panel.style.color = "white" ;
        panel.style.background = "red" ;
        start.disabled = true ;
        board.innerText = 0 ;
}
```

...cont'd

5 Add another function to specify element properties

```
function addScore( )
{
        var score = parseInt( board.innerText ) ;
        board.innerText = ++score ;
        if( score === 3 )
        {
                board.innerText += " ...Game Over!" ;
                panel.style.visibility = "hidden" ;
                start.disabled = false ;
        }
}
```

The text value of an element is a string data type. It must be converted to a number using the **parseInt( )** function so it can be increased – as described on pages 114-115.

6 Save the HTML document, then open it in your browser and click the components to change the element features

Don't get the same result? Check your code exactly matches the downloadable example source code – see page 6.

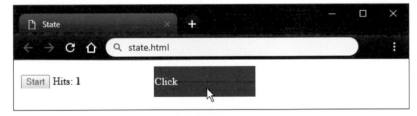

What you learned

- "DOM" stands for Document Object Model.

- The DOM is a family tree of the items on a web page.

- A **for-in** loop can list all properties of any DOM object.

- The DOM's top-level **window** object can be omitted in code, so **window.document** can be written simply as **document**.

- The **document.getElementById( )** method grabs a reference to a single element that has the **id** attribute value of its argument.

- The **document.getElementsByTagName( )** method grabs a reference to all elements having the tag name of its argument.

- The **document.getElementsByClassName( )** method grabs a reference to all elements having the class name of its argument.

- An **addEventListener( )** method can be added to an element reference to make the element respond to user actions.

- The **addEventListener( )** method needs two arguments to state the event type to listen for, and a function to call in response.

- An anonymous function has no name and can be given as the second argument to the **addEventListener( )** method.

- The **indexOf( )** method will return a positive integer only when its reference string contains its string argument.

- A function can be called after the web page loads by setting that function name to the DOM's **window.onload** property.

- Event listeners can be added in code to respond to "touch" events that occur in touchscreen devices.

- The **preventDefault( )** method of an event disables the usual behavior in response to "click" and "touchend" events.

- Element colors can be dynamically changed by setting new values to their **style.background** and **style.color** properties.

- Element states can be dynamically changed by setting new values to their **style.visibility** and **disabled** properties.

- Element content can be dynamically changed by setting new values to their **innerText** or **innerHTML** properties.

10 Put It All Together

Plan a web game

Before creating any web page it is useful to spend some time planning its design. Thinking ahead before you begin coding will save time later, as fewer tweaks will be needed to your web page.

It is generally helpful to consider these three key design points:

- **Purpose** – what exactly is your web page intended for?

- **Functionality** – what interactive functions will be needed to make your web page work for the user?

- **Components** – what elements will be needed on your web page to best present its content?

To demonstrate the process of building an interactive page from start to finish, the examples in this chapter will create a web page containing a variation of the popular "Whack-a-Mole" game.

Our version of the game will be entitled "Whack-a-Worm" (just to be a little different), and a plan for this web page might look like the design points listed on the opposite page.

Purpose

Display an interactive game in which images will appear briefly in different positions. The user must click or tap on an image when it's visible to advance a score counter until a limit is reached. The aim of the game is to hit every visible image to achieve the maximum possible score. The game will have the ability to be reset so the user may try again. The page will also provide a link to the author's website.

Functionality

- The ability to start and restart the game.

- The ability to select random positions.

- The ability to show and hide images.

- The ability to select random visible intervals.

- The ability to display the current hit score.

Components

- Heading to announce the game's name.

- Paragraph to briefly describe the game.

- List to provide instructions for the user.

- Table to provide cells for six image positions.

- Button to start and restart the game.

- Text to dynamically display the hit score.

- Footer to provide a link.

Create the outline

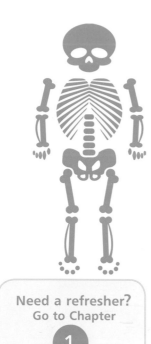

Need a refresher?
Go to Chapter
1

Having planned your web page design, as described on pages 140-141, you can begin to code your web page.

Begin by creating a barebones HTML document, as you did back on page 12, but also include elements where you can later add style sheet rules, division content, and JavaScript functions:

1 Launch your favorite plain text editor, then start a new document with the document type declaration
<!DOCTYPE HTML>

2 Below the document type declaration, add a root element that defines the document's language as English
<html lang="en" >

</html>

3 Within the HTML element, insert a head section
<head>

</head>

4 In the head section, insert elements defining the document's encoding character set, and add support for phone browsers – as you did back on page 19
<meta charset="UTF-8" >

<meta name="viewport"
content="width=device-width, initial-scale=1.0" >

5 Next, within the head section, insert an element defining the document's title
<title>Whack-a-Worm</title>

6 Now, within the head section, insert an element where you can add style rules later
<style>

</style>

7 After the head section, insert a document body section
<body>

</body>

8 Within the body section, insert an element where you can add content later
<div>

</div>

9 Next, in the body section, insert an element where you can add JavaScript functions later
<script>

</script>

10 Set the encoding to UTF-8, then save the document – your web page outline should look like this:

```
worm-barebones.html - Notepad                              —    □    ×
File  Edit  Format  View  Help
<!DOCTYPE HTML>

<html lang="en" >

<head>

<meta charset="UTF-8" >
<meta name="viewport" content="width=device-width, initial-scale=1.0" >
<title>Whack-a-Worm</title>

<style>

</style>

</head>

<body>

<div>

</div>

<script>

</script>

</body>

</html>
```

worm-barebones.html

> **Don't get the same result?** Check your code exactly matches the downloadable example source code – see page 6.

Announce the page

Having created a barebones HTML document, as described on pages 142-143, you can begin to add content to your web page.

You should first announce the page to the user by adding a most important heading, as you did back on page 20, in the page division created for content:

Need a refresher?
Go to Chapter

2

1 Copy the **worm-barebones.html** web page created in the previous example and rename it **worm-heading.html**

2 In the body of the document, add a heading element in the existing division element so it looks like this
<div>

<h1>Whack-a-Worm!</h1>

</div>

3 Save the HTML document, then open it in your desktop browser to see the title and heading displayed

worm-heading.html

4 Next, open the HTML document in a cellphone browser to see the heading displayed

5 Now, open the HTML document in a tablet browser to see the title and heading displayed

Don't get the same result? Check your code exactly matches the downloadable example source code – see page 6.

Describe the game

Having created the document heading, as described on pages 144-145, you can now add text content to your web page.

You can usefully add a paragraph, as you did back on page 22, providing a brief description of the page.

You can then add an unordered list, as you did back on page 33, providing instructions in bullet points:

Need a refresher?
Go to Chapter
3

1 Copy the **worm-heading.html** web page created in the previous example, and rename it **worm-text.html**

2 In the existing body section's division element, add a paragraph element so the division now looks like this
<div>

<h1>Whack-a-Worm!</h1>

<p>A challenging fun game of skill and speed.</p>

<!-- List to replace this comment. -->

</div>

3 Add this unordered list element in the division element
<ul>

<!-- List items to replace this comment. -->

</ul>

4 Now, add these list item elements within the unordered list element

<li>Worms will pop out of any hole TEN times</li>
<li>Whack as many as you can - you must be QUICK</li>
<li>Hit the START button to begin playing...</li>

5 Save the HTML document, then open it in your desktop browser, a cellphone browser, and tablet browser to see the paragraph and list displayed

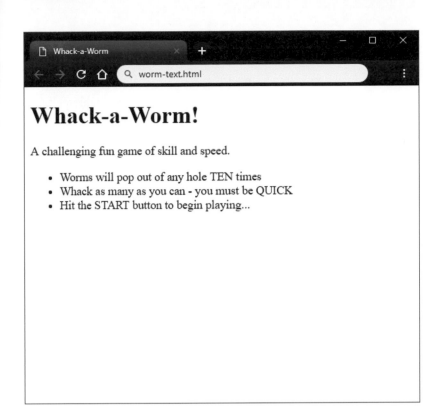

worm-text.html

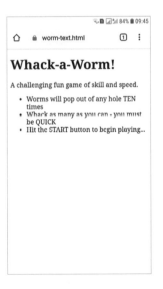

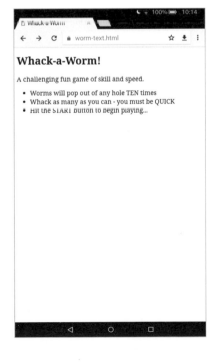

Don't get the same result? Check your code exactly matches the downloadable example source code – see page 6.

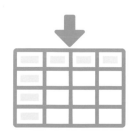

Need a refresher?
Go to Chapter
3

worm.png
(120px x 60px)
with transparent
background

Insert a table

Having provided a description and instructions, as described on pages 146-147, you can now add a game area to your web page.

You can add a table, as you did back on page 38, to contain the game components in individual table cells. Six of the table cells will each contain an image, and one table cell will contain a button and scoreboard text.

The table cells, images, button, and scoreboard elements must all include **class** or **id** attributes for styling and scripting:

1 Copy the **worm-text.html** web page created in the previous example, and rename it **worm-table.html**

2 In the existing body section's division element, add this 3-row table immediately below the instruction list

```
<table>

<tr>
<td class="hole" >
<img class="worm" src="worm.png" alt="Worm" ></td>
<td class="hole" >
<img class="worm" src="worm.png" alt="Worm" ></td>
<td class="hole" >
<img class="worm" src="worm.png" alt="Worm" ></td>
</tr>

<tr>
<td class="hole" >
<img class="worm" src="worm.png" alt="Worm" ></td>
<td class="hole" >
<img class="worm" src="worm.png" alt="Worm" ></td>
<td class="hole" >
<img class="worm" src="worm.png" alt="Worm" ></td>
</tr>

<tr>
<td class="rank" colspan="3" >
<button id="startButton" >Start</button>
Hits: <strong id="scoreBoard" >0</strong></td>
</tr>

</table>
```

3 Save the HTML document, then open it in your desktop, cellphone, and tablet browsers to see the table game area

...cont'd

worm-table.html

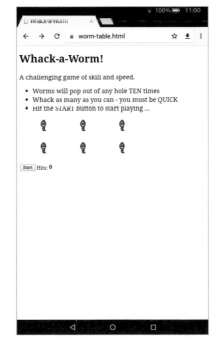

Don't get the same result? Check your code exactly matches the downloadable example source code – see page 6.

Add a footer

Having added a game area to your web page, as described on pages 148-149, you can now add a simple footer to the page.

To provide a footer you could insert a hyperlink, as you did back on page 28, pointing to the website of this web page's author:

Need a refresher?
Go to Chapter
2

1 Copy the **worm-table.html** web page created in the previous example and rename it **worm-footer.html**

2 In the existing body section's division element, add this paragraph immediately below the table
<p>Author:
<a href="https://www.ineasysteps.com" > In Easy Steps</a>
</p>

3 Save the HTML document, then open it in your desktop or cellphone browser and click the link to test it works

Validate your code

Having completed the HTML code you can now validate the document, as you did back on page 14, to ensure it has no errors:

1 Navigate to the W3C Validator Tool at **validator.w3.org**, then click on the "Validate by File Upload" tab

2 Click the "Choose File" button and select the document, then click the "Check" button to confirm it has no errors

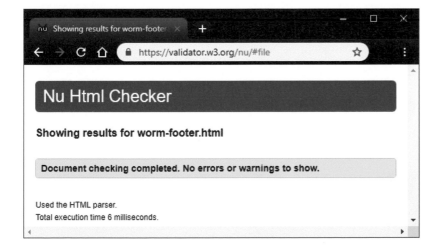

Need a refresher?
Go to Chapter

1

worm-footer.html

Don't get the same result? Check your code exactly matches the downloadable example source code – see page 6.

Make it stylish

Having completed and tested the HTML code of your web page, as described on page 151, you can now add a style sheet with rules to control the appearance of elements on the web page:

Need a refresher?
Go to Chapter

5

1 Copy the **worm-footer.html** web page created in the previous example and rename it **worm-style.html**

2 In the head section's style element, begin a style sheet by adding this rule to remove default browser style rules as you did on page 68

```
<style>
html,body        { margin:0px; padding:0px; border:0px  }
</style>
```

3 Next, in the style sheet, add this rule to specify the width and color of the page division, and to center it on the screen as you did back on page 69

```
div        { width:360px; color:brown; margin:auto }
```

4 Now, in the style sheet, add a rule to center the heading and paragraph text within the division element – also as you did on page 69

```
h1,p     { text-align:center }
```

5 Moving on to the game area, add a rule to the style sheet to set the table background color, and to remove default borders between each cell as you did back on page 72

```
table    { background:tan; border-collapse:collapse }
```

hole.png
(120px x 60px)
with transparent
background

6 Next, add this rule to set an image to be the background of selected cells – as you did back on page 71

```
td.hole { background:url( hole.png ) }
```

7 Now, add this rule to set the foreground and background color of other selected cells – also as you did on page 71

```
td.rank { background:brown; color:white }
```

8 Finally, add this rule to the style sheet to hide the foreground image in cells, as you did back on page 73, then open the HTML document in your browsers

```
img.worm        { visibility:hidden }
```

...cont'd

worm-style.html

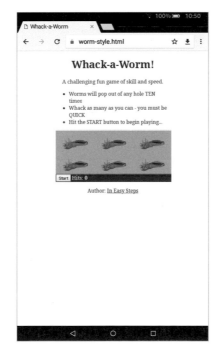

Don't get the same result? Check your code exactly matches the downloadable example source code – see page 6.

Begin the script

Having added styles to your web page, as described on pages 152-153, you can now begin to script some functionality.

You will first need to grab references to a few elements, as you did back on pages 128 and 129, so your script code can manipulate the game area. Event listeners can then be added, as you did on page 130, to respond to user actions.

Listen for both "click" and "touchend" events, as you did back on page 135, so your web page will work on touchscreen devices:

Need a refresher?
Go to Chapter
9

1. Copy the **worm-style.html** web page created in the previous example, and rename it **worm-listen.html**

2. In the body section's script element, begin a script by grabbing a reference to three elements
```
<script>
var worms = document.getElementsByClassName( "worm" ) ;
var board = document.getElementById( "scoreBoard" ) ;
var start = document.getElementById( "startButton" ) ;
</script>
```

3. Next, in the script, add an event listener to the button
```
start.addEventListener( "click" , startGame ) ;
```

4. Now, in the script, initialize a counter variable then write a loop to add event listeners to each image
```
var i = 0 ;

while( i < worms.length )
{
  worms[ i ].addEventListener( "mouseup", tapOrClick ) ;
  worms[ i ].addEventListener( "touchend", tapOrClick ) ;
  i++ ;
}
```

5. Add the function to prevent default behavior but respond when either a "click" or "touchend" event occurs
```
function tapOrClick( event )
{
  event.preventDefault( ) ;
  board.innerText = parseInt( board.innerText ) + 1 ;
  return false ;
}
```

This statement will show the number of times the user whacks the worm.

6 Finally, add the function to respond when the user clicks the button

```
function startGame( )
{
  start.disabled = true ;
  board.innerText = 0 ;
  alert( "Game Started" ) ;
}
```

This statement just tests that the event listener is working. It'll be replaced later with a statement to actually run the game.

7 Save the HTML document, then open it in your desktop and browsers – click or tap the button

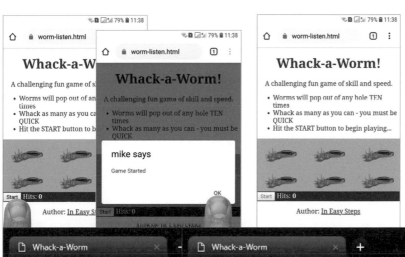

worm-listen.html

Don't get the same result? Check your code exactly matches the downloadable example source code – see page 6.

155

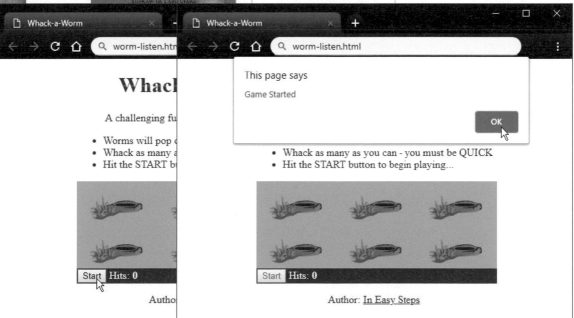

Continue the script

Having added event listeners to your web page, as described on pages 154-155, you can now manipulate elements of the page.

The game needs an image to appear briefly in different positions. This will be one of the table cells in which the foreground images are initially hidden.

You can select a random image using the **Math.random( )** method, as you did back on page 118, to choose an array index number. The image can then be revealed in its table cell by changing the image's visibility property from "hidden" to "visible":

Need a refresher?
Go to Chapter

8

Hot tip

This saved index number will be used later to ensure the image does not reappear in the same position when the function is called repeatedly.

1 Copy the **worm-listen.html** web page created in the previous example, and rename it **worm-random.html**

2 In the body section's script element, add a utility function that will return a random number within a specified range
```
function getRandom( min, max )
{
  return Math.floor( Math.random( ) * ( max - min ) + min ) ;
}
```

3 Next, add a function to get and store a random number, increase a counter, and pass the values to another function
```
function playGame( saved, counter )
{
  var index = getRandom( 0, worms.length ) ;

  saved = index ;
  counter++ ;

  showWorm( index, counter ) ;
}
```

Hot tip

This counter number will be used later to end the game after the worm image has appeared a set number of times.

4 Now, add a function to receive the passed values and reveal an image in one table cell
```
function showWorm( index, counter )
{
  worms[ index ].style.visibility="visible" ;
}
```

...cont'd

5 Finally, edit the existing function, created in Step 6 on page 155, to call a function to reveal an image in a cell

```
function startGame( )
{
  start.disabled = true ;
  board.innerText = 0 ;
  playGame( null, 0 ) ;
}
```

Don't get the same result? Check your code exactly matches the downloadable example source code – see page 6.

6 Save the HTML document, then open it in your desktop and cellphone browsers and click or tap the button to see an image – refresh the browser then repeat the action

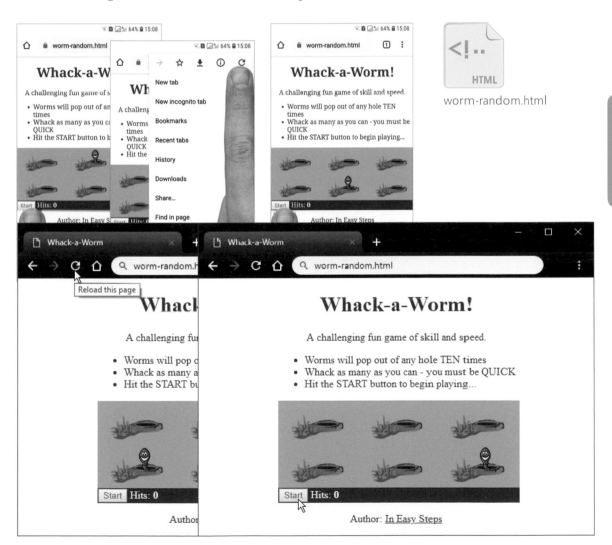

worm-random.html

Complete the script

Having created functions to reveal an image in a random location, as described on pages 156-157, you can now extend the functions to automate the process and so complete the web page.

A timer can be added, as you did back on page 120, to reveal an image at random positions for a specified number of times. The previous position can be examined by the timer to ensure the image will not appear at the same position it did the last time.

Each time the user clicks or taps a revealed image, the game score will increase by 1 and be displayed in the game area. When the timer ends, a notice will be added to the final game score:

Need a refresher?
Go to Chapter

8

HTML

worm.html

1 Copy the **worm-random.html** web page created in the previous example, and rename it **worm.html**

2 Edit the existing function, created in Step 3 on page 156, to examine the previously-saved random number and get a different random number

```
function playGame( saved, counter )
{
  var index = getRandom( 0, worms.length ) ;

  if( index === saved )
  {
    playGame( index, counter ) ;
  }
  else
  {

    // Nested if-else block to replace this comment.

  }

}
```

3 Next, insert a nested **if** block that will end the game after 10 images have been revealed

```
if ( counter > 9 )
{
  board.innerText += " ...Game Over!" ;
  start.disabled = false ;
  return true ;
}
// Else block to replace this comment.
```

4 Now, insert a nested **else** block to run the game if 10 images have not yet been revealed

```
else
{
  counter++ ;
  saved = index ;
  showWorm( index, counter ) ;
}
```

5 Turn your attention to the function created in Step 4 on page 156 that actually reveals an image

```
function showWorm( index, counter )
{
  worms[ index ].style.visibility="visible" ;

  // Timer to replace this comment.

}
```

6 Insert a timer to hide the currently-revealed image then reveal another image for 1 second (1000 milliseconds)

```
setTimeout(

  function( )
  {
    worms[ index ].style.visibility="hidden" ;
    playGame( index, counter ) ;
  } ,  1000
) ;
```

Don't forget

This is a statement, so it must end with a semicolon character.

7 To make the game play more interesting you can edit the timer above to vary the length of time for which an image is visible – let's say, between half a second and 1 second

```
setTimeout(

  function( )
  {
    worms[ index ].style.visibility="hidden" ;
    playGame( index, counter ) ;
  } ,  getRandom( 500, 1000 )
) ;
```

8 Save the HTML document, then open it in your desktop, tablet, or cellphone browser to play the web game

Play the web game

Having completed your web page, as described on pages 158-159, you can now test the game – and your reactions:

1 Press the "Start" button then click or tap the images as they appear to see if you can hit all 10

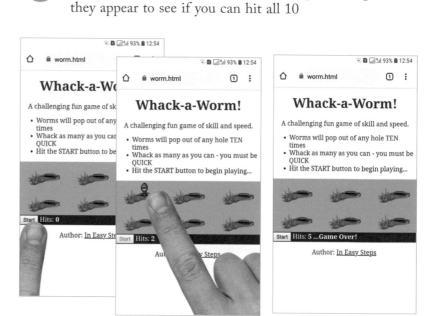

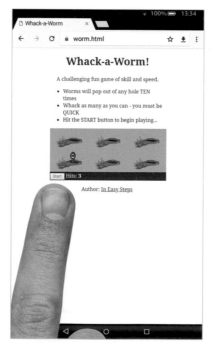

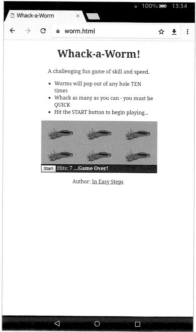

...cont'd

2 Not quick enough? Press the "Start" button once more to try again

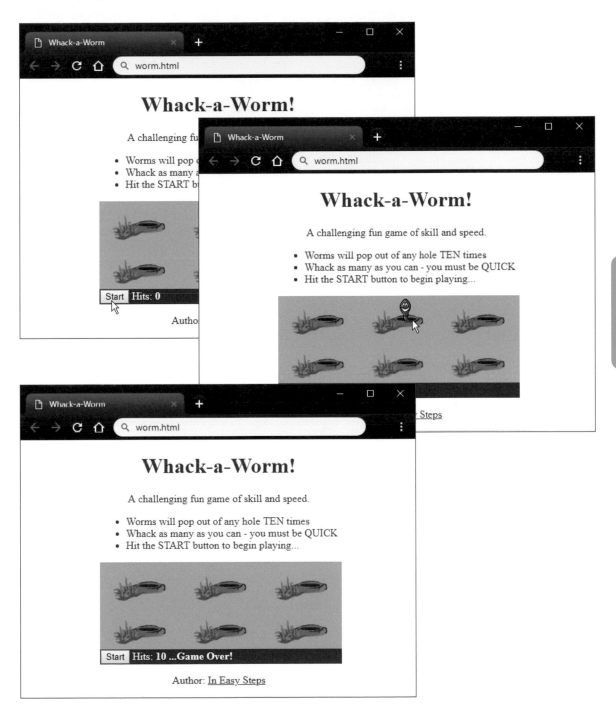

What you learned

- When designing a web page it is useful to consider its precise purpose, needed functionality, and required components.

- Elements for content, style sheet rules, and JavaScript functions can be added to a barebones HTML document.

- The most important heading at the top of a web page announces the page to the user.

- An initial paragraph can describe the web page.

- An unordered list can be used to provide instructions in bullet points.

- A table can be used to contain game components in individual table cells.

- Elements containing game components can include **class** or **id** attributes for styling and scripting.

- A web page footer can provide a hyperlink pointing to the website of the web page's author.

- After completing and testing the HTML code of a web page, style sheet rules can be added to control elements' appearance.

- A style sheet can begin with a rule to remove default browser style rules affecting margins and other spacing.

- A script can begin with statements that grab references to those elements to be manipulated by the script code.

- Event listeners can listen for both "click" and "touchend" events so the web page will work on touchscreen devices.

- Script can select a random element in an array by using the **Math.random( )** method to choose an array index number.

- A hidden element can be revealed by changing its visibility property from "hidden" to "visible".

- A timer can be used to reveal and hide an element a specified number of times.

- A variable within a function can store a previously-selected number to ensure that number is not used when next called.

+ Handy Reference

HTML fundamental tags

The HTML tags in the table below are the fundamental tags needed to create a valid "barebones" web page document:

Element:	Description:
<!DOCTYPE>	Document type declaration tag. The very first element in each document, defining the HTML markup version being used. Empty element – no closing tag required
Attributes:	**HTML** – Required to identify the markup version as HTML5 and so set the browser to "Standards Mode"
<html>	HTML tag. The "root" element that encloses the entire head and body sections of the document
Attributes:	**lang** – Content language by standard abbreviation Example: **lang="en"** (English)
<head>	Head tag. Encloses elements that provide information about the document, such as title, metadata, style sheet, etc.
Attributes:	-
<meta>	Metadata tag. Specifies information about the document defined by its attributes. Empty element – no closing tag required
Attributes:	**charset** – Specifies the character encoding used by the document, such as "UTF-8"
<title>	Title tag. Encloses text that is the title of the HTML document
Attributes:	-
<body>	Body tag. Encloses the entire contents of the document including text, hyperlinks, images, tables, lists, etc.
Attributes:	**onload** – Specifies script to run when the document loads into the web browser

Useful comments can be added to the HTML web page code using the special tag below:

Element:	Description:
<!-- -->	Comment tag. Encloses text comments that are ignored by the browser. Empty element – no closing tag required
Attributes:	-

A valid barebones HTML document containing a comment and the fundamental tags looks like this:

```
<!DOCTYPE HTML>

<html lang = "en" >


<head>

<meta charset = "UTF-8" >

<title>Basic Web Page</title>

</head>


<body>

<!-- Comment: content to replace this element. -->

</body>


</html>
```

You can check that your HTML documents are valid using the W3C Markup Validation Service online at **validator.w3.org.**

HTML content tags

The HTML tags in the table below are used to add simple content to a web page document:

Element:	Description:
\<div\>	Division tag. Encloses a group of other elements for styling purposes only
Attributes:	-
\<h1\> \<h2\> \<h3\> \<h4\> \<h5\> \<h6\>	Heading tags. Encloses text to appear as document or section headings, ranked by prominence where **\<h1\>** has the highest rank and **\<h6\>** has the lowest
Attributes:	-
\<p\>	Paragraph tag. Encloses text and automatically adds space before and after itself to create a paragraph block
Attributes:	-
\<img\>	Image tag. Inserts an image into the document. Empty element – no closing tag required
Attributes:	**src** – Specifies the URL of the image **width** – Specifies the image width **height** – Specifies the image height **alt** – Specifies a required alternative text description of the image **usemap** – Specifies the name of a map to be used with this image
\<br\>	Break tag. Inserts a single line break. Empty element – no closing tag required
Attributes:	-
\<hr\>	Horizontal Rule tag. Inserts a horizontal ruled line between differing content. Empty element – no closing tag required
Attributes:	-

The HTML tags in the table below are used to enhance text content in a web page document:

Element:	Description:
<b>	Bold tag. Encloses content that is to be displayed in a bold font
Attributes:	-
<i>	Italics tag. Encloses content that is to be displayed in an italic font
Attributes:	-
<strong>	Strong tag. Encloses text that should be considered to be important
Attributes:	-
<em>	Emphasis tag. Encloses text that should be displayed in an emphasized manner
Attributes:	-

Below is a division that encloses a heading and a paragraph containing text enhancements, line breaks, and an image:

```
<div>

<h1>Page Announcement</h1>

<p>

<strong> This is an important line</strong>
<br>but<br>
<em>this is an emphasized line.</em> <br>

<img  src="exciting-picture.png"
      width="500" height="375"
      alt="An Exciting Picture" >
</p>

</div>
```

HTML list tags

The HTML tags in the table below are used to add lists to a web page document:

Element:	Description:
<ul>	Unordered List tag. Encloses list item elements to define an unordered list
Attributes:	-
<ol>	Ordered List tag. Encloses list item elements to define an ordered list
Attributes:	**start** – Specifies the number at which to begin the numbering
<li>	List Item tag. Encloses text that is an item in an unordered or ordered list
Attributes:	-
<dl>	Definition List tag. Encloses definition description and definition term tags to create a definition list
Attributes:	-
<dt>	Definition Term tag. Encloses a definition term within a definition list
Attributes:	-
<dd>	Definition Description tag. Encloses the description of a definition term within a definition list
Attributes:	-

An unordered list provides bullet points for each list item and looks like this:

```
<ul>
<li>First point</li>
<li>Second point</li>
<li>Third point</li>
</ul>
```

An ordered list provides numbering for each list item and looks like this:

```
<ol>
<li>First item</li>
<li>Second item</li>
<li>Third item</li>
</ol>
```

A definition list provides a definition description for each list term and looks like this:

```
<dl>
<dt>First term</dt>   <dd>Definition of first term</dd>
<dt>Second term</dt> <dd>Definition of second term</dd>
<dt>Third term</dt>  <dd>Definition of third term</dd>
</ul>
```

HTML table tags

The HTML tags in the table below are used to add tables to a web page document:

Element:	Description:
<table>	Table tag. Encloses table component elements such as caption, table row, table header, and table data cells
Attributes:	-
<caption>	Caption tag. Encloses a table caption. If included it must immediately follow the opening **<table>** tag
Attributes:	-
<tr>	Table Row tag. Encloses table header or data cell elements, to define an entire table row
Attributes:	-
<th>	Table Heading tag. Encloses text that is to be displayed as a column or row heading
Attributes:	**colspan** – Specifies the number of columns the heading cell should span **rowspan** – Specifies the number of rows the heading cell should span
<td>	Table Data tag. Encloses text data that is to be displayed in a regular table data cell
Attributes:	**colspan** – Specifies the number of columns the table data cell should span **rowspan** – Specifies the number of rows the table data cell should span

...cont'd

A simple captioned table looks like this:

```
<table>
<caption>Simple Table</caption>
<tr> <td>A1</td>    <td>A2</td>    <td>A3</td> </tr>
<tr> <td>B1</td>    <td>B2</td>    <td>B3</td> </tr>
<tr> <td>C1</td>    <td>C2</td>    <td>C3</td> </tr>
</table>
```

Cells that span rows or columns must contain the same number of cells as unspanned rows and columns. Below is a table with column and row headers and cells that span columns and rows:

```
<table>
<tr> <th></th> <th>Column 1</th> <th>Column 2</th> </tr>
<tr> <th>Row A</th><td>A1</td>    <td>A2</td> </tr>
<tr> <th>Row B</th> <td colspan="2" >A1 + A2</td> </tr>
<tr> <th>Row C</th> <td rowspan="2" >C1 + D1</td>
                                <td>C2</td> </tr>
<tr> <th>Row D</th> <td>D2</td> </tr>
</table>
```

HTML interactive tags

The HTML tags in the table below are used to add interactive components to a web page document:

Element:	Description:
\<button>	Button tag. Encloses text to appear on a user-activated button
Attributes:	-
\<a>	Anchor tag. Encloses a hyperlink, or acts as a placeholder
Attributes:	**href** – Specifies the URL address of a hyperlink target
\<map>	Map tag. Encloses a number of area elements to define an image map
Attributes:	**name** – Specifies a unique map name
\<area>	Area tag. Specifies an area of an image map defined by its attributes. Empty element – no closing tag required
Attributes:	**alt** – Specifies alternative text like a tooltip **shape** – Defines the area shape **coords** – States the area's XY coordinates

HTML inclusion tags

The HTML tags in the table below are used to include style rules and JavaScript code in a web page document:

Element:	Description:
\<style>	Style tag. Encloses style rules, to define a CSS style sheet
Attributes:	-
\<script>	Script tag. Encloses JavaScript code, or specifies an external script resource
Attributes:	**src** – Specifies the URL address of a script file processed after the page loads

HTML global attributes

The attributes in the table below may each be included in any HTML element – these are known as "global" attributes:

Attribute:	Specifies:
class	One or more space-separated class names Example: class = "recipes fish"
id	Unique identity name for the element Example: id = "item_22"
lang	Content language by standard abbreviation Example: lang = "en" (English)
style	One or more CSS style rules Example: style = "border:2px solid red"
title	Advisory information such as a Tooltip Example: title = "Click or Tap Here"

HTML event attributes

The attributes in the table below may each be included in any HTML content element to respond to mouse action events:

Attribute:	Specifies:
onclick	Script code to run when the user clicks on the element content
onmouseover	Script code to run when the user positions the mouse pointer over the element content
onmouseout	Script code to run when the user moves the mouse pointer off the element content
onmousedown	Script code to run when the user presses a mouse button while the mouse pointer is over the element content
onmouseup	Script code to run when the user releases a mouse button while the mouse pointer is over the element content

CSS selectors & properties

A CSS style rule begins with a selector, followed by a declaration block containing one or more declarations that each specify a property and a valid value for that property, and looks like this:

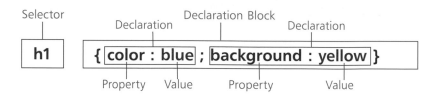

The common CSS selectors that are featured in this book are listed in the table below:

Name:	Targets:	Example:
Type	Any element of a specified type defined by tag name	p { color : green }
Group	Multiple elements of the specified types defined by tag name	h1, h2, h3 { color : green }
Class	The name assigned to a class attribute using dot notation	p.grn { color : green }
ID	The name assigned to an id attribute using hash notation	p#grn { color : green }

Useful comments can be added to a CSS style sheet using the special symbols below:

Symbols:	Description:
/* */	Comment block. Encloses text comments that are ignored by the browser. The comment can be one single line or spread over multiple lines, but must begin with /* and end with */

The useful properties in the table below appear in the CSS style
rules featured in this book:

Property:	Specifies:
margin	Size of the area outside an element. This can be specified as a fixed number of pixels or to automatically center an element within its outer container Example: **margin:20px** Example: **margin:auto**
padding	Size of area to add inside an element Example: **padding:5px**
border	Width, and optionally, border type and color Example: **border:0px** Example: **border:3px solid red**
width	Width of an element Example: **width:360px**
height	Height of an element Example: **height:270px**
color	Foreground color for text content Example: **color:red**
background	Background color of an element or a background image of an element Example: **background:tan** Example: **background:url(image.png)**
font	Font size and font family, and optionally, font style and font weight Example: **font:large sans-serif** Example: **font:italic bold large sans-serif**
visibility	Displays or hides the element Example: **visibility:visible** Example: **visibility:hidden**
text-align	Positions text content horizontally Example: **text-align:center**
vertical-align	Positions text content vertically Example: **vertical-align:middle**

JavaScript keywords

Keywords, reserved words, and object names that must be avoided when choosing names in JavaScript are listed below:

Keywords:					
break	case	catch	continue	default	delete
do	else	false	finally	for	function
if	in	instanceof	new	null	return
switch	this	throw	true	try	typeof
var	void	while	with		

Reserved words:				
abstract	boolean	byte	char	class
const	debugger	double	enum	export
extends	final	float	goto	implements
import	int	interface	long	native
package	private	protected	public	short
static	super	synchronized	throws	transient
volatile				

Objects:				
Array	Date	Math	Object	String
window	location	history	navigator	document
images	links	forms	elements	XMLHttpRequest

- The **var** keyword is used to create a JavaScript variable in which to store data.

- The **true** and **false** keywords are Boolean values, which can be represented numerically as **1** (true) and **0** (false).

- The **null** keyword represents a value of absolutely nothing – not even an empty string or zero.

- The **this** keyword references the object to which it belongs.

JavaScript operators

The symbols that have special meaning in JavaScript are listed in the table below:

Operator:	Description:
=	Assignment
+=	Addition and assignment
;	Statement terminator
<	Less Than comparison
<=	Less Than or Equal comparison
>	More Than comparison
>=	More Than or Equal comparison
===	Equality comparison
!==	Inequality comparison
++	Increment (+1)
--	Decrement (-1)
[ ]	Array index
( )	Set precedence
+	Addition (add numbers)
+	Concatenation (join strings)
-	Subtraction
-=	Subtraction and assignment
*	Multiplication
*=	Multiplication and assignment
/	Division
/=	Division and assignment
%	Modulus (division remainder)
%=	Modulus and assignment
//	Single-line comment
/* */	Multiple-line comment
&&	Logical AND
||	Logical OR
!	Logical NOT

JavaScript structures

The basic conditional test that determines the direction of flow in a script looks like this:

```
if ( condition )
{
        statement/s-to-execute-when-true ;
}
```

The basic conditional test can be extended to provide an alternative direction of flow looks like this:

```
if ( condition )
{
        statement/s-to-execute-when-true ;
}
else
{
        statement/s-to-execute-when-false ;
}
```

Multiple conditional tests can be made to provide several alternative directions of flow, like this:

```
if ( condition )
{
        statement/s-to-execute-when-true ;
}
else if ( condition )
{
        statement/s-to-execute-when-true ;
}
else if ( condition )
{
        statement/s-to-execute-when-true ;
}
else
{
        statement/s-to-execute-when-false ;
}
```

A loop to repeatedly execute statements while a conditional test remains true looks like this:

```
while ( condition )
{
        statement/s-to-execute-when-true ;

        statement-to-change-the-conditional-test-result ;
}
```

A basic function block to execute the statements it contains whenever the function gets called in the script looks like this:

```
function function-name ( )
{
        statement/s-to-execute ;
}
```

A function that provides parameters so the caller can pass in values for use by the function's statements looks like this:

```
function function-name ( parameter-name , parameter-name )
{
        statement/s-to-execute ;
}
```

A function that provides parameters and returns a value to the caller looks like this:

```
function function-name ( parameter-name , parameter-name )
{
        statement/s-to-execute ;

        return value-to-be-returned ;
}
```

JavaScript built-in functions

The built-in functions listed in the table below are used to display a dialog box on a web page:

Function:	Description:
alert(*string*)	Displays a message dialog containing the string argument and an OK button
confirm(*string*)	Displays a message dialog containing the string argument, plus an OK button and a Cancel button. Returns **true** if the user clicks OK otherwise it returns **false**
prompt(*string*)	Displays an input dialog containing the string argument, plus an OK button and a Cancel button. Returns input if the user clicks OK otherwise it returns **null**

The built-in functions listed in the table below are used to manipulate strings and numbers:

Function:	Description:
parseInt(*string*)	Returns an integer from the beginning of the string argument if possible, otherwise it returns **NaN** (not a number)
parseFloat(*string*)	Returns a floating point number from the beginning of the string argument if possible, otherwise it returns **NaN**
isNaN(*argument*)	Returns **true** if the specified argument is not a number, otherwise it returns **false**
number.toString( )	Returns a string data type version of the specified number

The built-in **Date** object provides many methods to manipulate date and time strings. These are listed and described on page 112.

...cont'd

The built-in functions listed in the table below are used to create and cancel timer events on a web page:

Function:	Description:
setTimeout(*fcn, ms*)	Calls a specified function after a specified number of milliseconds Example: **var timer = setTimeout(greet , 3000) ;** calls **greet( )** after 3 seconds
clearTimeout(*timer*)	Clears a specified timer created with the **setTimeout( )** function

The built-in **Math** object provides the methods listed in the table below that are used to manipulate numbers:

Function:	Description:
Math.round(*number* **)**	Returns the nearest integer to the specified number
Math.floor(*number* **)**	Returns the integer immediately below the specified number
Math.cell(*number* **)**	Returns the integer immediately above the specified number
Math.max(*num, num* **)**	Returns the larger of the two specified numbers
Math.min(*num, num* **)**	Returns the smaller of the two specified numbers
Math.random( )	Returns a random floating-point number between zero and (up to but not including) one Example: **Math.floor(Math.random( ) * 10) ;** returns an integer from 0 to 9

DOM properties & methods

The **Element** object of the Document Object Model (DOM) represents an HTML element and includes the useful properties listed in the table below:

Property:	Description:
element.tagName	Returns the tag name of the element in all uppercase characters Note that this property is readonly Example: **<button onclick="alert(this.tagName)" >** returns the string "BUTTON"
element.id	Returns the value assigned to the element's **id** attribute. This property can also be used to assign an id value Example: *element*.id = "unique-id"
element.className	Returns the value assigned to the element's **class** attribute. This property can also be used to assign one or more class names to an element Example: *element*.className = "one two"
element.innerText	Returns the text content of an element. This property can also be used to assign text to an element Example: *element*.innerText = "Demo"
element.innerHTML	Returns the text and HTML content of an element. This property can also be used to assign text and HTML tags Example: *element*.innerHTML = "Demo"
element.disabled	Returns **true** for a disabled interactive element, or returns **false** if it is enabled This property can also be used to disable and enable interactive elements Example: *element*.disabled = true
element.style	Returns a **Style** object that has properties representing CSS styles. This can be used to get current style values or set new style value. Example: *element*.style.visibility = "hidden"

The **Element** object of the Document Object Model (DOM) represents an HTML element and provides the useful methods listed in the table below:

Method:	Description:
element.**addEventListener(** *event* , *function* **)** Attaches a specified event-handler function to an element to respond when the specified event occurs Example: **function handler( ) { alert("Click Detected") ; }** *event*.**addEventListener(** "click" , **handler)**	
element.**preventDefault( )**	Cancels an event so that the element's default action will not be performed

The **document** object of the Document Object Model (DOM) represents the root element of an HTML document and provides the useful methods listed in the table below:

Method:	Description:
document.getElementById(*string* **)** Returns a reference to the single element that has the specified string value assigned to its id attribute Example: **var elem = document.getElementById(** "unique-id" **)**	
document.getElementsByTagName(*string* **)** Returns a reference to all elements of the specified tag name. Each element can be addressed by its index number Example: **var para = document.getElementsByTagName(** "p" **)** here **para[0]** addresses the first paragraph element	
document.getElementsByClassName(*string* **)** Returns a reference to all elements of the specified class name. Each element can be addressed by its index number Example: **var ones = document.getElementsByClassName(** "one" **)** here **ones[0]** addresses the first element of the "one" class	

Hexadecimal color codes

The colors that can be assigned to elements of a web page can be described by their name or by a code number. The code number contains a **#** hash character and six letters or numbers. These are three pairs of values, in the hexadecimal numbering system between **00** (0) and **FF** (255). Each pair represents the Red, Green, and Blue component intensity within the color – the higher the number, the greater the intensity. For example, **#FF0000** is maximum red, comprising Red (255), Green (0), and Blue (0).

The following tables list the color names, as shown on page 64, together with their equivalent color code:

Decimal:	Hex:
0	00
1	01
2	02
3	03
4	04
5	05
6	06
7	07
8	08
9	09
10	0A
11	0B
12	0C
13	0D
14	0E
15	0F
16	10
17	11
18	12
19	13
20	14
21	15
22	16
23	17
24	18

Name:	Code:
AliceBlue	#F0F8FF
AntiqueWhite	#FAEBD7
Aqua	#00FFFF
Aquamarine	#7FFFD4
Azure	#F0FFFF
Beige	#F5F5DC
Bisque	#FFE4C4
Black	#000000
BlanchedAlmond	#FFEBCD
Blue	#0000FF
BlueViolet	#8A2BE2
Brown	#A52A2A
BurlyWood	#DEB887
CadetBlue	#5F9EA0
Chartreuse	#7FFF00
Chocolate	#D2691E
Coral	#FF7F50
CornflowerBlue	#6495ED
Cornsilk	#FFF8DC
Crimson	#DC143C
Cyan	#00FFFF
DarkBlue	#00008B

Name:	Code:
DarkCyan	#008B8B
DarkGoldenRod	#B8860B
DarkGray	#A9A9A9
DarkGreen	#006400
DarkKhaki	#BDB76B
DarkMagenta	#8B008B
DarkOliveGreen	#556B2F
DarkOrange	#FF8C00
DarkOrchid	#9932CC
DarkRed	#8B0000
DarkSalmon	#E9967A
DarkSeaGreen	#8FBC8F
DarkSlateBlue	#483D8B
DarkSlateGray	#2F4F4F
DarkTurquoise	#00CED1
DarkViolet	#9400D3
DeepPink	#FF1493
DeepSkyBlue	#00BFFF
DimGray	#696969
DodgerBlue	#1E90FF
FireBrick	#B22222
FloralWhite	#FFFAF0
ForestGreen	#228B22
Fuchsia	#FF00FF
Gainsboro	#DCDCDC
GhostWhite	#F8F8FF
Gold	#FFD700
GoldenRod	#DAA520
Gray	#808080
Green	#008000
GreenYellow	#ADFF2F

Name:	Code:
HoneyDew	#F0FFF0
HotPink	#FF69B4
IndianRed	#CD5C5C
Indigo	#4B0082
Ivory	#FFFFF0
Khaki	#F0E68C
Lavender	#E6E6FA
LavenderBlush	#FFF0F5
LawnGreen	#7CFC00
LemonChiffon	#FFFACD
LightBlue	#ADD8E6
LightCoral	#F08080
LightCyan	#E0FFFF
LightGoldenRodYellow	#FAFAD2
LightGray	#D3D3D3
LightGreen	#90EE90
LightPink	#FFB6C1
LightSalmon	#FFA07A
LightSeaGreen	#20B2AA
LightSkyBlue	#87CEFA
LightSlateGray	#778899
LightSteelBlue	#B0C4DE
LightYellow	#FFFFE0
Lime	#00FF00
LimeGreen	#32CD32
Linen	#FAF0E6
Magenta	#FF00FF
Maroon	#800000
MediumAquaMarine	#66CDAA
MediumBlue	#0000CD
MediumOrchid	#BA55D3

...cont'd

Name:	Code:
MediumPurple	#9370DB
MediumSeaGreen	#3CB371
MediumSlateBlue	#7B68EE
MediumSpringGreen	#00FA9A
MediumTurquoise	#48D1CC
MediumVioletRed	#C71585
MidnightBlue	#191970
MintCream	#F5FFFA
MistyRose	#FFE4E1
Moccasin	#FFE4B5
NavajoWhite	#FFDEAD
Navy	#000080
OldLace	#FDF5E6
Olive	#808000
OliveDrab	#6B8E23
Orange	#FFA500
OrangeRed	#FF4500
Orchid	#DA70D6
PaleGoldenRod	#EEE8AA
PaleGreen	#98FB98
PaleTurquoise	#AFEEEE
PaleVioletRed	#DB7093
PapayaWhip	#FFEFD5
PeachPuff	#FFDAB9
Peru	#CD853F
Pink	#FFC0CB
Plum	#DDA0DD
PowderBlue	#B0E0E6
Purple	#800080
RebeccaPurple	#663399
Red	#FF0000

Name:	Code:
RosyBrown	#BC8F8F
RoyalBlue	#4169E1
SaddleBrown	#8B4513
Salmon	#FA8072
SandyBrown	#F4A460
SeaGreen	#2E8B57
SeaShell	#FFF5EE
Sienna	#A0522D
Silver	#C0C0C0
SkyBlue	#87CEEB
SlateBlue	#6A5ACD
SlateGray	#708090
Snow	#FFFAFA
SpringGreen	#00FF7F
SteelBlue	#4682B4
Tan	#D2B48C
Teal	#008080
Thistle	#D8BFD8
Tomato	#FF6347
Turquoise	#40E0D0
Violet	#EE82EE
Wheat	#F5DEB3
White	#FFFFFF
WhiteSmoke	#F5F5F5
Yellow	#FFFF00
YellowGreen	#9ACD32

Index